Eyes Open 2

WORKBOOK
with Digital Pack

Vicki Anderson with **Eoin Higgins**

CAMBRIDGE
UNIVERSITY PRESS

Discovery
EDUCATION

Contents

Starter Unit

Family

1 ★ **Put the letters in order to make family words.**

1 umm   _mum_
2 dda   _____
3 madrang   _____
4 enrpast   _____
5 leunc   _____
6 rtborhe   _____
7 fewi   _____
8 trisse   _____
9 natu   _____
10 sicuno   _____
11 dradngad   _____
12 baunsdh   _____

2 ★★ **Match the words in Exercise 1 to make pairs.**

1 wife – _husband_
2 uncle – _____
3 grandma – _____
4 dad – _____
5 brother – _____

3 ★★★ **Complete the definitions.**

1 My mum and dad are my _parents_ .
2 My aunt's husband is my _____ .
3 My granddad's wife is my _____ .
4 My aunt's children are my _____ .
5 My grandma and granddad are my _____ .
6 My dad's wife is my _____ .
7 My mum and dad's child is my _____ or _____ .

Subject pronouns and *be*

4 ★ Circle **the correct options.**

1 Where am **I** / **you**?
2 **Is** / **Are** you from Canada?
3 Daniel **am** / **is** my cousin. **He** / **They** is 14.
4 My sister's birthday **are** / **is** in May.
5 My grandparents **are** / **is** in Japan. **She's** / **They're** on holiday.
6 My brother and I **am** / **are** at the zoo. **We** / **They** are not at school.
7 I **am** / **is** at the cinema. Are **you** / **he** at the shops?

be

5 ★★ **Complete the sentences and questions with the correct form of *be*.**

1 _Are_ you at home?
2 This _____ my mum.
3 We _____ best friends.
4 _____ they from England?
5 His sister _____ in my class.
6 I _____ from Edinburgh, Scotland.
7 _____ you in the school football team?
8 My new dog _____ called Bob.

Possessive *'s*

6 ★ **Complete the sentences with *'s* in the correct place.**

1 My mum ‸_'s_ car is red.
2 Our cousin house is in the city.
3 Is this your granddad piano?
4 What's your dad name?
5 My best friend birthday is in October.
6 His sister dance classes are on Monday.
7 Is our dog nose brown?
8 Where is my brother T-shirt?

Starter Unit

School subjects

1 ★★ Look at the pictures and complete the crossword with the school subjects.

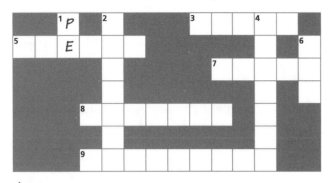

down

across

2 ★★ Match the school subjects with the sentences.

> ICT Geography French ~~History~~
> Maths PE Science English Music

1 'Let's talk about the year 1914.'   _History_
2 'What does *je m'appelle* mean?'   _____
3 'OK, run around the gym ten times.'   _____
4 'Turn on the computers, please.'   _____
5 'Let's play it again and listen to
   the piano.'   _____
6 'Water is hydrogen and … what?'   _____
7 'What is 15 x 14?'   _____
8 'Where are the Rocky Mountains?'   _____
9 'Let's look at the verb *to be*.'   _____

there is/*are* and *some* and *any*

3 ★★ Find five more differences between Picture A and Picture B and write sentences. Use *there is(n't)* / *there are(n't)*.

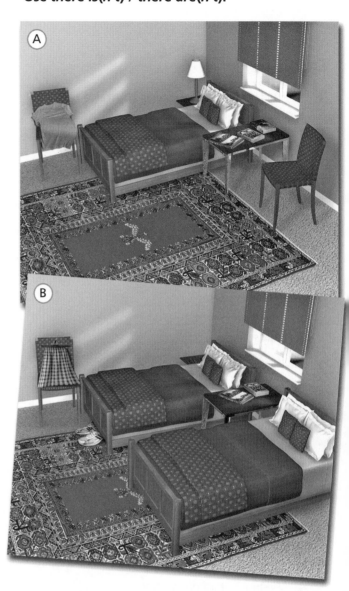

1 _In Picture A there are three books. In Picture B_
   there are two.
2 _____
   _____
3 _____
   _____
4 _____
   _____
5 _____
   _____
6 _____
   _____

Starter Unit

1 ★★ (Circle) the correct options and complete the sentences with *some* or *any*.

1 There (isn't) / aren't ____any____ cheese in the fridge.
2 Are / Is there _____ giraffes in the zoo?
3 Is there / Are there _____ T-shirts in your bag?
4 There is / are _____ fruit in the kitchen.
5 There isn't / aren't _____ boats on the river.
6 Is there / Are there _____ pasta in the cupboard?
7 There is / are _____ good photos on your mobile phone.
8 There isn't / aren't _____ money in my bag.

have got

2 ★ (Circle) the correct options.

1 I ('ve) / 's got a new computer.
2 Have / Has you got a mobile phone?
3 My sister have / has got a TV in her room.
4 We 've / 's got a pet cat. His name is Peru.
5 Have / Has he got your phone number?
6 They 've / 's got two houses in the city.
7 She haven't / hasn't got a brother.
8 Our dog 've / 's got a tennis ball.
9 We haven't / hasn't got a big family.

Sports and activities

3 ★★ Put the letters in order to make sports and activities. Then complete the sentences with the correct form of *play*, *do* or *go*.

1 Do you ____play____ ____basketball____ at your school? (sblaltabke)
2 I'd like to _____ _____ in the evenings. (gyoa)
3 We _____ _____ in the mountains every winter. (gisnki)
4 Can you _____ _____? (yalolblelv)
5 My brother _____ _____ every Saturday. (duoj)
6 A lot of people _____ _____ in the sea in Ireland. (fnruisg)
7 My family sometimes _____ _____ in the lake. (mgnswmii)
8 Let's _____ _____ at the skate park later. (aasgbtdkineor)
9 Do you often _____ _____ with your friends? (libogwn)
10 I want to _____ _____ but my brother's got my bike. (liccgyn)

Present simple: affirmative and negative

4 ★ (Circle) the correct words in the grammar table.

1	I/You/We/They **watch / watches** TV.
2	He/She/It **finish / finishes** at five.
3	We **don't / doesn't** like carrots.
4	She **don't / doesn't** like bananas.

5 ★★ Complete the text with the present simple form of the verbs in brackets.

My family ¹____loves____ (love) sport. We all ²_____ (play) one sport or more. My dad ³_____ (play) tennis every Saturday. My mum ⁴_____ (go) to the gym and ⁵_____ (do) yoga twice a week. I ⁶_____ (do) karate after school and every weekend I ⁷_____ (go) skateboarding with friends. My brother ⁸_____ (play) basketball and he ⁹_____ (train) four days a week. We often ¹⁰_____ (go) to see him play. We ¹¹_____ (not watch) sport on TV because we ¹²_____ (not like) watching TV.

Starter Unit

Present simple: *Yes/No* questions

1 ★ (Circle) the correct words in the grammar table.

1	**Do you / You** like karate?
2	Yes, I **do / does**. No, I **don't / doesn't**.
3	**He / Does he** play tennis?
4	Yes, he **do / does**. No, he **don't / doesn't**.

2 ★★ Complete the questions and answers with the correct form of *do*.

1 _____Do_____ you do your homework in the evening? Yes, I _____do_____ .

2 _____ Harry and Gina go cycling on Saturdays? No, they _____ .

3 _____ Nina like Geography? No, she _____ .

4 _____ your friends go skateboarding? Yes, they _____ .

5 _____ they use the Internet to study French? No, they _____ .

6 _____ your brother do karate? Yes, he _____ .

7 _____ your teacher show videos in English class? No, she _____ .

Present simple: *Wh-* questions

3 ★★ Match the question words with the words in the box.

person   object/thing   place   ~~frequency~~   time   reason

1	how often *frequency*	4	where	_____
2	what	_____	5	who	_____
3	when	_____	6	why	_____

4 ★★ Complete the questions with the correct question word from the box.

How often   What   When   ~~Where~~   Who   Why   Where

1 **A:** ___*Where do you live?*___ (you / live)
  B: In London.

2 **A:** _____ does he study?
  B: English and Maths.

3 **A:** _____ do they play sports?
  B: Once a week.

4 **A:** _____ does he go cycling with?
  B: His brother.

5 **A:** _____ do you like skateboarding?
  B: Because it's fun.

6 **A:** _____ does she play volleyball?
  B: In the park.

7 **A:** _____ does he go to drama class?
  B: On Saturdays.

Adverbs of frequency

5 ★ (Circle) the correct words in the grammar table.

1	Going swimming with my friends **is always / always is** good fun.
2	We **go sometimes / sometimes go** to the sports centre on Saturdays.

6 ★★ Put the words in the correct order to make sentences.

1 football / play / school / at / We / always
  We always play football at school.

2 Football / sometimes / matches / long / are / very
  _____

3 never / me / with / My dad / chess / plays
  _____

4 We / often / Saturdays / on / go / cycling
  _____

5 dictionaries / use / English class / usually / We / in
  _____

6 are / His / really interesting / books / always
  _____

Vocabulary

Shops

1 ★ **Find ten shops in the word search.**

e	l	s	p	o	r	t	s	o	c	d
l	c	v	e	n	m	o	s	o	h	e
e	p	r	d	z	u	s	h	y	e	p
c	b	m	t	h	s	x	o	o	m	a
t	g	l	d	e	i	n	e	u	i	r
r	q	j	b	d	c	t	e	r	s	t
o	b	o	o	k	s	h	o	p	t	m
n	p	l	c	e	u	w	z	m	e	e
i	v	c	l	o	t	h	e	s	t	n
c	n	e	i	l	r	m	e	r	p	t
s	u	p	e	r	m	a	r	k	e	t
s	n	e	w	s	a	g	e	n	t	b

2 ★ **Complete the table with the words from Exercise 1.**

1 Five words that go with *shop*	
___*sports*___ shop	_____ shop
_____ shop	_____ shop
_____ shop	
2 One word that goes with *store*	
_____ store	
3 Four words that are <u>ONE</u> word	
_____	_____
_____	_____

3 ★★ **Complete the sentences with words from Exercise 1.**

1 You can buy trainers and boots in a *shoe shop* .
2 I need some aspirin from the _____ .
3 My favourite shop is the _____ because it sells magazines and chocolate.
4 I like that _____ because it's got great T-shirts and cheap jeans.
5 I'd like to look at some laptops – let's go to the _____ .
6 Why don't you go to the _____ to buy a book for your dad's birthday?
7 We're going to the _____ to buy fruit, vegetables and some other things.
8 I like the guitars in this _____ .

4 ★★ **Complete the text with words from Exercise 1.**

There is a shopping centre in my town, but my friends and I don't often go there. It's got a [1] *newsagent* where you can buy magazines or birthday cards, and a couple of [2]_____ with jeans and T-shirts, but nothing cool for teenagers. My mum and dad love the [3]_____ because you can find everything you need there. There are some shops I like. There's a [4]_____ with great trainers, and there's also an [5]_____ with lots of tablets and smartphones, but they're a bit expensive. My favourite is the [6]_____ because it plays all the new songs, and a lot of young people go there.

5 ★★★ **Write about a shopping centre you know. Complete the sentences about it.**

1 It's got a *big department store* .
2 There's a _____ where you can buy _____ and _____ .
3 I like the _____ because it's got _____ .
4 I don't go to the _____ because it hasn't got _____ .
5 My mum and dad like the _____ because _____ .

Language focus 1

Present continuous

1 ★ Circle the correct words in the grammar table.

1	She**'s looking** / **looking** at boots in the shoe shop.
2	They **not buying** / **aren't buying** those T-shirts.
3	**Are you coming** / **You are coming** with us?
4	Yes, **I'm** / **I am**. No, we **aren't** / **isn't**.
5	To talk about facts, habits and routines, use the present **simple** / **continuous**.
6	To talk about an action in progress, use the present **simple** / **continuous**.

2 ★★ Complete the conversations with the present continuous form of the verbs in brackets.

> **Joe:** Hi Bob. We're [1] ___meeting___ (meet) outside the shopping centre. Where are you?
> **Bob:** I [2] _____ (sit) on the bus. Where are you?
> **Joe:** Outside the shopping centre. Ian and I [3] _____ (wait) for you now.
> **Bob:** OK. There's a lot of traffic. The bus [4] _____ (not go) very fast.
> **Joe:** Well, we [5] _____ (not stay) here a long time. It's cold! Where's the bus now?
> **Bob:** It [6] _____ (come) into Mill Street, so see you in two minutes.

3 ★★ Complete the questions and short answers with the correct form of the present continuous. Use the words in the box.

> you sell   we have   ~~he look~~
> you spend   they buy   Lisa wait

1 ___Is he looking for a book in English?___
   ___Yes, he is.___
2 _____ your old video games?
   Yes, _____ , for €5 each.
3 _____ that CD?
   No, _____ .
4 _____ lunch now?
   No, _____ , just a drink.
5 _____ in the café?
   No, _____ . She's late.
6 _____ £20 on a T-shirt?
   Yes, _____ . It's a present.

Present simple vs. continuous

4 ★★ Circle the correct words in the text.

My sister and I [1]**try** / **are trying** an experiment at the moment – no shopping for a month! Usually Mum [2]**gives** / **is giving** me pocket money on Saturday and my friends and I [3]**go** / **are going** shopping in the afternoon, but this Saturday is different. My friends [4]**shop** / **are shopping** for clothes and things but I [5]**write** / **'m writing** this blog at home. Why? Well, I [6]**have** / **am having** a lot of things that I never [7]**wear** / **am wearing**. This month my sister Jane and I [8]**put** / **are putting** our pocket money in our money boxes for our holidays, and we [9]**do** / **are doing** lots of other things. Shopping all the time is boring!

5 ★★★ Write the questions in the present simple or present continuous and answer them for you.

1 What / wear / at the moment?
   What are you wearing at the moment?
   I'm wearing ...
2 you / reading / a good book / at the moment?
   _____
   _____
3 Where / usually / buy your clothes?
   _____
   _____
4 you / listen to music? What / you / listen to?
   _____
   _____

Explore extreme adjectives

6 ★★ Complete the definitions with the adjectives in the box.

> huge   ~~great~~   wonderful   amazing
> brilliant   boiling   awful   freezing

1 When something is very good we say it's
   ___great___ , _____ , _____ or
   _____ .
2 When it's very hot, we say it's _____ .
3 When something is very big, we say it's
   _____ .
4 When it's very cold, we say it's _____ .
5 When something is very bad, we say it's
   _____ .

Listening and vocabulary

Money verbs

1 ★ **Match the verbs in the box with the correct definition.**

```
sell   spend   save   earn   buy   borrow
```

1 get money from working   _earn_
2 get money from someone to keep
   for a short time   _____
3 what a shop does   _____
4 pay money to get something specific   _____
5 use money for something, not only
   in shops   _____
6 keep money so you can use it in
   the future   _____

2 ★★ **Complete the sentences with the verbs from Exercise 1.**

1 I'm trying to ____save____ my pocket money for a
   new smartphone.
2 Jane wants to _____ all her video games
   for €10 each.
3 Can I _____ €5 from you until tomorrow?
4 Some people _____ a lot of money on
   clothes.
5 How much money does a shop assistant
   _____ ?
6 I want to _____ some new skates this year.

3 ★★★ **Write the answers to the questions. Use the present continuous and the words in brackets.**

1 What are you doing on ebay? (sell / my computer)
   I'm selling my computer.
2 Why are you putting money in that box? (save
   for / new bike)
   _____
3 Why are you going to Helen's house? (borrow /
   her dress)
   _____
4 Why are you in the sports shop? (buy / new
   trainers)
   _____
5 What are you doing? (spend / five pounds /
   sweets!)
   _____
6 Why are you cleaning your dad's car? (earn /
   money / a new phone)
   _____

Listening

4 ★ 🔊 **01 Listen to the conversation between Gemma and her mum. What is Gemma's problem?** (Circle) **the correct option.**
a clothes   b money   c her brother

5 ★★ 🔊 **01 Read the sentences. Listen again and circle the correct options.**

1 Gemma wants to buy a pair of jeans (online) /
   at the shopping centre.
2 Gemma's pocket money is **£50 / £30** a month.
3 **Gemma / Gemma's brother** saves money.
4 Gemma says she needs more money than her
   brother because **she's older / he only buys
   video games**.
5 The cinema costs **£5 / £10**.
6 Her mum tells Gemma to **do work in their
   house / get a babysitting job**.
7 Gemma **likes / doesn't like** her mum's idea.
8 Gemma's mum gives her **more money / a job**.

Language focus 2

(don't) want to, would(n't) like to, would prefer to

1 ★ Circle the correct options.

1 **Would** / **Do** you like to save more money?
2 Would you **prefer** / **want** the black T-shirt or the white one?
3 I'd **want** / **like** to go to the electronics shop to see some new mobile phones.
4 She **doesn't want** / **wouldn't prefer** to borrow money from her sister.
5 Would you **like** / **want** to go to the bookshop?
6 I **wouldn't like** / **don't prefer** to buy a new car.

2 ★ Match the questions with the answers.

1 Does your friend want to come with us?   _c_
2 Would you like to listen to music?   ___
3 Would Barry prefer to go to the sports shop?   ___
4 Do they want to invite Paul to come shopping?   ___
5 Would Mary and Arthur like to go to a café?   ___
6 Would Claudia prefer to do the exam today?   ___

a Yes, he would.   d Yes, she would.
b No, they wouldn't.   e Yes, I would.
c No, she doesn't.   f Yes, they do.

3 ★★ Complete the sentences with the correct form of the verbs in the box.

> sell   spend   play   g̶o̶   earn   buy

1 I don't want ___to go___ to a bookshop.
2 We'd really like _____ more money.
3 I wouldn't like _____ a lot of money on a phone.
4 Yolanda would prefer not _____ some new trainers.
5 They want _____ video games.

4 ★★★ Complete the sentences with your own ideas.

1 I'd prefer to eat …
_____ .
2 I wouldn't like to be …
_____ .
3 I don't want to go …
_____ .
4 I really want to be …
_____ .
5 In the future I would …
_____ .

(not) enough + noun

5 ★★ Match the sentence beginnings (1–6) with the sentence endings (a–f).

1 We can't make a cake because …   _e_
2 They're not dancing here because …   ___
3 I can't do all my homework because …   ___
4 A lot of people were still hungry because …   ___
5 We can't all study for the exam because …   ___
6 We want to buy a new tablet but …   ___

a … there wasn't enough food.
b … we haven't got enough money.
c … there isn't enough space.
d … I haven't got enough time.
e … there aren't enough eggs.
f … there aren't enough books.

6 ★★★ Read the problems and write a sentence with (*not*) *enough*.

1 There are five T-shirts in the shop and 20 people want to buy one.
**There aren't enough T-shirts in the shop.**

2 I've got £20 and these jeans cost £15.
_____

3 There are a lot of children in this town and there's only one small park.
_____

4 We've got 10 bottles of water for 100 people.
_____

5 She's got 30 minutes before her class to do this exercise.
_____

6 We're going to make sandwiches for 30 people but we've only got 25 slices of bread.
_____

 Explore adjective prefixes

7 ★★ Add the prefix *un-* to the adjectives and match them with the definitions.

> friendly   h̶a̶p̶p̶y̶   usual   tidy   fair   helpful

1 sad   _unhappy_
2 different or not common   _____
3 not nice to another person   _____
4 not wanting to help someone   _____
5 when the rules are not the same for everyone   _____
6 when things are not clean or not in the right place   _____

Reading

1 ★ **Read the text about a new supermarket. What is different about it?**

SHOPPING BY PHONE

On the walls of an underground station in central Seoul, South Korea, there are a lot of pictures of food and drinks: bananas, meat, rice, coffee, even pet food. But these are not **advertisements**. This is the world's first 'virtual' supermarket, called *Homeplus*.

The supermarket is unusual because you use the special *Homeplus* app on your smartphone to go shopping. When you want to buy something, you use this **app** to scan the barcodes of the products you want. You put them in your online **shopping trolley** and then you pay by phone. You haven't got any heavy bags to carry because the supermarket **delivers** everything to your house for you.

South Koreans like shopping online and millions of them have smartphones, but are they ready for this type of shopping? 'Young Koreans use their smartphones to do a lot of different **tasks** every day,' says a *Homeplus* virtual store manager. 'Our customers work really hard and don't have enough time to go to the supermarket. Our store helps them save time.' So, is this the future?

2 ★★ **Complete the definitions with the words in bold from the text.**

1 ___*Tasks*___ are little jobs we do every day at work or at home.
2 Sometimes in the middle of a TV programme, they show _____ .
3 An _____ is a small computer program on your phone or tablet.
4 When you call a pizza company, it normally _____ the pizzas to your house.
5 A _____ is something you put your food in at the supermarket.

3 ★★ **Read the text again. Answer the questions.**

1 Where is the supermarket?
   ___It's in an underground station in Seoul.___
2 What can you buy at the supermarket?
   _____
3 What do you need to buy things here?
   _____
4 What happens after you pay for your shopping?
   _____
5 Why does the store manager think it's good for Koreans?
   _____

4 ★★★ **Complete the advertisement for *Homeplus* with words from the text.**

HOMEPLUS
– the virtual supermarket

We help you save time!
1 Choose the f___*ood*___ or d___*rink*___ you want.
2 Scan the b_____ .
3 Fill your s_____ t_____ with food.
4 P_____ for your shopping with your p_____ .
5 *Homeplus* d_____ everything to your house.

5 ★★★ **What's good about a virtual shop like this? What's bad about it? Write at least five sentences.**

_____
_____
_____
_____
_____

Writing

An email

1 Read Jenny's email. What is her problem with money?

Hi Gina,
I get £5 a week pocket money, but I spend it all. How can I save my money?
Please help!
Jenny

Hi Jenny,
I have the same problem! Try writing down everything you buy for a week and how much it costs. Do you spend a lot on food and drink, for example? Don't spend money on things you don't need. Make a sandwich at home, and don't buy sweets every day.
Put some money in your money box when you get it. Ask for five £1 coins so you can do this. Sometimes I try to earn some money from my family. Maybe you can do jobs, for example, wash the car or water the plants. But be realistic – £5 isn't a lot!
Good luck,
Gina

2 Complete the table with Gina's advice.

Do	Don't
write down everything you buy for a week	

Useful language Imperatives _____

3 Look back at Gina's email. Write the positive and negative imperatives that go before these words.
1 _____Try_____ writing down
2 _____ spend money
3 _____ sweets every day
4 _____ for five £1 coins
5 _____ realistic

4 Put the words in order to make sentences.
1 saving / every / Try / week / something
Try saving something every week.
2 extra money / work / Do / at home / some / to earn
_____
3 things / Don't / silly / money / on / spend
_____
4 extra money / things / Try / to get / selling
_____
5 borrow / friends / from / Don't / your / money
_____

Writing

> **WRITING TIP**
>
> Make it better! ✓ ✓ ✓
> Use *and*, *or*, *but* and *so* to make your sentences longer.
> *I buy sweets **and** chocolate.*
> *I earn lots of money **but** I spend it all!*
> *I'd like to go to Australia **so** I'm saving my pocket money.*

5 **Complete the sentences with *and, or, but,* or *so*.**

1 Don't spend all your pocket money ____so____ you can save some every week.
2 Don't buy sweets, water _____ sandwiches.
3 Make your own sandwich _____ bring your own water.
4 Try selling some books _____ CDs.
5 I get £5 a week _____ I spend it all!

6 **Complete the sentences with the correct preposition.**

1 Don't spend a lot of money ____on____ sweets.
2 Ask _____ your pocket money in coins.
3 Don't borrow money _____ your friends.
4 Would you like to sell this _____ me?
5 I'm trying to save money _____ my holidays.

> **WRITING TIP**
>
> Make it better! ✓ ✓ ✓
> If a friend has a problem, say you understand and wish them good luck.
> *I understand your problem. Best of luck with it.*

7 **Read the sentences. Which ones say you understand (*U*) and which wish someone good luck (*GL*)?**

1 I hope this works for you.   *GL*
2 I totally understand the problem.   ____
3 That happens to me too!   ____
4 Best of luck.   ____
5 I wish you luck.   ____

8 **Read Gina's email again and tick (✓) the information she includes.**

Things not to do	✓
A friendly comment to start the email	☐
A nice way to finish the email	☐
Own experience	☐
Suggestions about what to do	☐
Asking for more information	☐
A reason why something is/isn't a good idea	☐

PLAN

9 **Read the question in the email below. Use the information in Exercise 8 and make notes.**

Hi everyone,
I want to earn some money for my summer holidays.
I need some ideas!
Thanks,
Freddie.

WRITE

10 **Write an email. Look at page 17 of the Student's Book to help you.**

_____
_____
_____
_____
_____
_____
_____
_____
_____
_____
_____
_____
_____
_____

CHECK

11 **Check your writing. Can you say YES to these questions?**

- Is the information from Exercise 8 in your description?
- Do you start by saying you understand and end by wishing them luck?
- Are there positive and negative imperatives?
- Do you join sentences with *and, or, but* or *so*?
- Do you use the correct prepositions?
- Are the spelling and punctuation correct?

Do you need to write a second draft?

Vocabulary
Shops

1 Circle the correct options.
1 A bookshop sells **books** / sweets.
2 A chemist sells **medicine** / newspapers.
3 A newsagent sells **shoes** / comics.
4 A sports shop sells **trainers** / books.
5 A music shop sells **guitars** / computers.
6 An electronics shop sells **laptops** / CDs.
7 A supermarket sells **food and drink** / pianos.
8 A shoe shop sells **posters** / shoes.
9 A department store **has got** / hasn't got electronics.
10 A clothes shop sells **shirts** / cheese.

Total: 9

Money verbs

2 Complete the text with the verbs in the box.

spend save earn ~~sell~~ buy borrow

I want to ¹____*sell*____ my old computer and ²_____ a new one. I ³_____ some of my money every week because I don't usually ⁴_____ all of my pocket money. At the weekend, I ⁵_____ money doing jobs in the garden for our neighbours. I can also ⁶_____ some money from my mum and pay it back later.

Total: 5

Language focus
Present continuous

3 Complete the conversation with the present continuous form of the verbs in the box.

drink leave not answer not work
buy ~~wait~~ walk eat

Joe: Where are you? We ¹_*'re waiting*_ for you in the café.
Tom: I ²_____ a CD for you.
Joe: That's nice of you! Thanks! I ³_____ hot chocolate at the moment and Sarah ⁴_____ a cake.
Tom: Where's Peter? He ⁵_____ his phone.
Joe: That's because his phone ⁶_____ . He's here. He ⁷_____ into the café right now.
Tom: Great! I ⁸_____ the shop now. See you in a bit.

Total: 7

Present simple vs. continuous

4 Complete the text with the correct form of the verbs in brackets.

I usually ¹____*go*____ (go) shopping with my friends on Saturdays. My sister ²_____ (not go) with us. She usually ³_____ (go) to her friend's house. But today we ⁴_____ (not go) anywhere. We ⁵_____ (stay) at home. My sister ⁶_____ (make) a cake. I ⁷_____ (write) in my blog and Mum ⁸_____ (listen) to music. We ⁹_____ (not spend) a lot of time together at home. We sometimes ¹⁰_____ (talk) to each other only by phone or text! So today we ¹¹_____ (do) something different. It's a nice change!

Total: 10

(don't) want to, would(n't) like to, would prefer to

5 Complete the sentences with *want*, *like* or *prefer*.
1 **A:** Do you ____*want*____ to go shopping?
  B: I don't like shopping. I'd _____ to play volleyball.
2 **A:** Would you _____ to go cycling on Saturday?
  B: No, I _____ to stay at home and play video games.
3 **A:** Do you _____ to save money?
  B: Yes, but I'd also _____ to buy a new computer!
4 **A:** I think I'd _____ to sell my bicycle.
  B: Great because I _____ to buy it!
5 **A:** I haven't got enough money. I'd _____ to borrow some from you but I'd _____ not to pay it back until next month.
  B: What? No way!

Total: 9

(not) enough + noun

6 Complete the sentences with *enough* and the words in the box.

> people money ~~food~~ cheese homework time

1 I want to make lunch for my friends but we haven't got _enough food_ .
2 My parents would like to go snowboarding this year but they haven't got _____ .
3 I need to call my grandma this morning but I haven't got _____ .
4 We'd like to start a school volleyball team but we haven't got _____ .
5 Have we got _____ to make a pizza?
6 The teacher is angry because the students don't do _____ .

☐ Total: 5

Language builder

7 ⟨Circle⟩ the correct words.

> **Gina:** I ¹_____ my new trainers today. Do you ²_____ them?
> **Chris:** They're great. I need ³_____ trainers. Where ⁴_____ them?
> **Gina:** I ⁵_____ them online. How about you?
> **Chris:** I ⁶_____ to the sports shop in town. I ⁷_____ in town on Saturdays and there's a shop on my way home.
> **Gina:** Have you got ⁸_____ pairs of trainers?
> **Chris:** Only two. I haven't got ⁹_____ to buy more. I ¹⁰_____ to buy another pair.
> **Gina:** Me too!
> **Chris:** But you ¹¹_____ a new pair!
> **Gina:** Oh yeah!

1	**a** wear	**ⓑ** 'm wearing	
2	**a** likes	**b** like	
3	**a** some	**b** any	
4	**a** do you buy	**b** you buy	
5	**a** usually buy	**b** buy usually	
6	**a** sometimes go	**b** go sometimes	
7	**a** often am	**b** am often	
8	**a** much	**b** many	
9	**a** enough money	**b** money enough	
10	**a** like	**b** 'd like	
11	**a** wear	**b** 're wearing	

☐ Total: 10

Vocabulary builder

8 Complete the table with the words in the box.

> ~~spend~~ newsagent bowling bookshop save borrow skiing chemist cycling yoga earn supermarket department store basketball buy skateboarding karate sell

Sports	Shops	Money verbs
		spend

☐ Total: 17

Speaking

9 ⟨Circle⟩ the correct options.

> **Martina:** Excuse me, ¹⟨I'd like⟩ / I like to buy a T-shirt.
> **Shop assistant:** What ²size / number are you?
> **Martina:** I'm a small.
> **Shop assistant:** What about this one?
> **Martina:** I'd ³want / prefer a red one.
> **Shop assistant:** A red one? Here you ⁴be / are.
> **Martina:** Can I try it on?
> **Shop assistant:** Yes, sure. … How is it?
> **Martina:** It's great. How ⁵much / money is it?
> **Shop assistant:** It's €6.99.
> **Martina:** ⁶I take / 'll take it.

☐ Total: 5

☐ Total: 77

Present simple vs. continuous

Remember that:

- we use the present simple to talk about facts, habits and routines.
- we use adverbs of frequency with the present simple.
- we use the present continuous to talk about actions in progress at the time of speaking.
- we use *at the moment* and *(right) now* with the present continuous.

1 Correct the incorrect sentences.

1 At the weekend, I'm often going shopping.
At the weekend, I often go shopping.

2 I'm helping Mum in the kitchen right now.
_____

3 Alex isn't here – he visits a friend at the moment.
_____

4 I've got some important news! Are you listening?
_____

5 In my country, we are drinking a lot of tea.
_____

(don't) want to, would(n't) like to, would prefer to

Remember that:

- we use the infinitive with *to* after **want**, **would like** and **would prefer**.
  ✓ **I would like to go** shopping.
  ✗ *I would like going shopping.*
- we use **would**, not *do*, to make questions with **would like** and **would prefer**, but we use **do** to make questions with **want**.
  ✓ **Would you like** to come to the supermarket?
  ✗ *Do you like to come to the supermarket?*

2 Circle the correct words.

Jack: Hi, Emily. ¹ **Do** / (**Would**) you like to come shopping with me? I want ² **buy** / **to buy** some new clothes for my holiday.

Emily: OK. But I ³ **don't** / **not** want to go to the shopping centre in town. I ⁴ **would** / **will** prefer to go to the department store. It has better clothes.

Jack: OK. We can walk to the department store, or would you ⁵ **want** / **prefer** to go by bike?

Emily: Well, I think I'd like ⁶ **going** / **to go** by bike.

Jack: Is 3 o'clock OK? Or ⁷ **will** / **would** you prefer to go a bit later?

Emily: Yes, 3 o'clock is fine. See you then! Bye!

Extreme adjectives

Remember that:

- we use **very** to make adjectives stronger.
- we don't usually use **very** before extreme adjectives.
  ✓ It's **very hot** in July, but in August it's **absolutely boiling**!
  ✗ *It's absolutely hot in July, but in August it's very boiling!*

3 Match the sentence halves.

1 Our holiday in England was absolutely …   *f*
2 I'm watching the new *Batman* film. It's very … ___
3 Let's go to the beach. It's absolutely … ___
4 The new shopping centre is very … ___
5 My friend's new bedroom is absolutely … ___
6 Open the window. It's very … ___

a … big.   d … boiling!
b … huge!   e … good.
c … hot in here.   f … amazing!

Spell it right! The *-ing* form

Remember that:

- for verbs ending in *-e*, we remove the *e* before we add *-ing*: give → **giving**.
- for verbs ending with one vowel and one consonant, we double the final consonant: shop → **shopping**.
- for verbs ending in *-y*, we just add *-ing*: study → **studying**.

4 Complete the sentences with the correct *-ing* form of the verb in brackets. Check your spelling!

1 We can't play football today. It's ____*raining*____ . (rain)
2 She's _____ a letter to her penfriend. (write)
3 We go _____ every day in the holidays. I love it! (swim)
4 I don't like _____ video games. Let's go outside. (play)
5 They enjoy _____ to music on their smartphones. (listen)
6 Kim and Julie are going _____ this afternoon. (shop)
7 They're _____ new clothes for their holidays. (buy)
8 They're _____ for their holiday in Greece. (save)

2 Our heroes

Vocabulary

Jobs

1 ⭐ **Find nine more jobs in the word search.**

a	s	t	m	u	m	o	t	e	r	l	w	a
c	w	r	u	b	j	u	p	i	b	d	l	s
r	e	i	s	y	o	l	k	s	e	a	n	t
p	o	l	i	c	e	o	f	f	i	c	e	r
a	l	o	c	n	g	v	f	i	l	t	m	o
d	a	f	i	t	r	e	c	r	y	o	k	n
l	i	n	a	k	u	t	h	e	s	r	t	a
w	e	s	n	u	r	s	e	f	m	o	n	u
o	d	f	b	n	u	l	s	i	e	v	e	t
c	a	h	t	r	i	w	e	g	o	p	e	r
i	n	p	o	l	r	v	e	h	a	c	r	e
s	c	i	e	n	t	i	s	t	n	o	r	s
j	e	y	o	n	e	c	h	e	r	t	h	l
q	r	z	u	i	m	x	a	r	t	i	s	t

2 ⭐⭐ **Circle the correct words in the conversation.**

A: What do you want to do when you leave school?

B: I want to be rich and famous! When I was little, I wanted to be an ¹**artist / astronaut** and travel to the moon, or a ²**vet / nurse** and save animals' lives or work in a zoo!

A: Oh, so what are you good at?

B: Not a lot! I like acting, but I'm not very good and I can't play the guitar.

A: So you don't want to be a ³**musician / firefighter** or ⁴**an actor / a police officer**?

B: No! I don't think so. I don't think I'm very creative.

A: Well, what about a ⁵**nurse / scientist** – then you can help people get better.

B: No, I think that's a difficult job. I'd really like to be ⁶**an artist / a dancer** and paint beautiful pictures.

3 ⭐⭐⭐ **Complete the definitions with the words from Exercise 1.**

1 They move to music. You can see them in the theatre or at a concert. *dancer*

2 They find people who do bad things. _____

3 They play the guitar, the piano or another instrument. _____

4 You can see them in the theatre, on TV or in films. _____

5 They work in a hospital, helping doctors. _____

6 They paint pictures or make beautiful things. _____

7 They help animals when they're sick. _____

8 They travel to space and they sometimes stay there for a few months. _____

9 They study and work in universities or laboratories. _____

10 They help people when a building is on fire. _____

4 ⭐⭐⭐ **Choose two or three jobs. What is good about them? What isn't very good? Write at least five sentences.**

It's a very interesting job. A scientist needs to study for a long time.

_____

_____

_____

_____

_____

Language focus 1

was/were

1 ★ (Circle) the correct words.

1	I/He/She/It **was / were** there.
2	You/We/They **was / were** there.
3	I/He/She/It **wasn't / weren't** there.
4	You/We/They **wasn't / weren't** there.

2 ★★ **Complete the sentences with *was* or *were* (✓), *wasn't* or *weren't* (✗).**

1 We _____were_____ (✓) both in the hockey team, but you _____ (✓) a good player and I _____ (✗) very good.

2 Bill Gates and Paul Allen _____ (✗) interested in finishing their university studies. They _____ (✓) only interested in computers.

3 Before he _____ (✓) an actor, Hugh Jackman _____ (✓) a PE teacher at a school.

4 Kaká _____ (✓) always a good footballer and his brother, Digão, _____ (✓) just like him. They _____ (✓) both very good footballers but Kaká _____ (✓) better.

Past simple: affirmative and negative

3 ★ (Circle) the correct words.

1	I/You/He/She/It/We/They **staying / stayed** there.
2	I/You/He/She/It/We/They **didn't stay / didn't stayed** there.
3	I/You/He/She/It/We/They **didn't go / didn't went** there.

4 ★★ **Complete the newspaper story with the past tense form of the verbs in the box.**

be	not be	~~drop~~	not find	go	have	not have
look	open	phone	pick	say	see	take

Six months ago 15-year-old Courtney Barwick
[1] _*dropped*_ her wallet outside a restaurant. When
she got home, she [2]_____ for it in her bag, but it
[3]_____ there. Courtney went to the restaurant,
but she [4]_____ the wallet. She didn't expect
to see it again, but she was lucky. Someone saw it,
[5]_____ it up and [6]_____ it to a bank.
The wallet [7]_____ Courtney's phone number
in it, so the bank [8]_____ her to tell her they
had her wallet. The next day, she [9]_____ to the
bank to get it. When she [10]_____ the wallet,
she [11]_____ $20 inside it, and a note. The note
[12]_____ 'Surprise!' and it [13]_____
a surprise, because when Courtney lost her wallet, it
[14]_____ any money in it!

5 ★★★ **Your friend Paul lost something last week. Answer the questions with full sentences using the words in brackets.**

1 What did he lose? (tablet)
He lost his tablet.

2 When did he lose it? (last Friday)
_____

3 What happened? (leave / on the bus)
_____

4 Did he find it again? How? (Yes / the driver / pick it up)
_____

5 How did he get it back? (go / bus station / get it)
_____

Time expressions

6 ★★ **Order the sentences with time expressions. Start with the most recent.**

a I went to the shop yesterday. ___

b I did my homework this morning. _1_

c They couldn't play the piano when they were little. ___

d My parents visited Rome four days ago. ___

e They went snowboarding last month. ___

(E)xplore expressions with *make*

7 ★★ **Match the sentence beginnings (1–6) with the sentence endings (a–f).**

1 My homework was really bad   _c_

2 I like cooking so I sometimes help   ___

3 When I was at summer camp last year,   ___

4 OK, you don't know what to do,   ___

5 I want to do something amazing   ___

6 Before you go out,   ___

a I made lots of friends.

b so I can make history.

c because I made a lot of mistakes.

d so can I make a suggestion?

e make sure you do your homework.

f my mum to make a cake.

Listening and vocabulary

Adjectives of character

1 ★ Use the clues to complete the crossword.

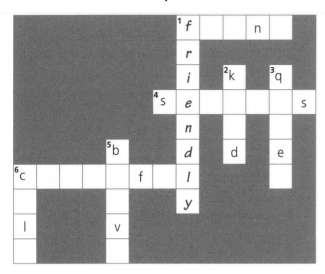

across

1 She always makes people laugh.
4 He didn't laugh or smile at all.
6 She is always happy and smiling.

down

1 The new student talked to lots of people.
2 He gave me some of his food.
3 Mark didn't say anything all evening.
5 Ellen wasn't afraid of the snake.
6 My friend never gets stressed.

2 ★★ Circle the correct words.

My two best friends are Chris and Adam. They are very different. Chris and I are always laughing because he is very ¹funny / brave, but Adam is very ²cheerful / serious. He doesn't smile much. A lot of people think he is unhappy but he isn't, he's quite ³cheerful / kind really! He is also a very ⁴brave / quiet person, especially at school, where he doesn't talk much. Chris is the opposite. He's ⁵friendly / calm to everyone and never stops talking! I'm not good at Science like they are, but they are both really ⁶kind / serious and help me with my homework or before an exam. Last term I was nervous before a Physics exam! Chris and Adam never panic. They told me to be ⁷friendly / brave, stay ⁸quiet / calm, and do the exam. And they were right, it wasn't a difficult exam and I passed!

Listening

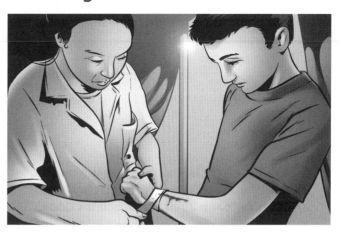

3 ★★ 🔊 02 Listen to the radio interview with a teenager called Jonah. What happened to him? Circle the correct option.

a He was ill on a survival course.
b He saved his friend from the river.
c He survived a bear attack.

4 ★★ 🔊 02 Listen again. Circle the correct words.

1 Two / Three teenagers were injured in a bear attack.
2 They were on a survival course in Alaska / Australia.
3 When the attack happened, the teenagers were walking / camping.
4 The accident happened before / after dinner.
5 When Jonah saw the bear, he did / didn't do what the instructors said.
6 The attack was very fast / slow.
7 The rescue helicopter arrived that night / in the morning.
8 Tracey Smith was a teacher / a student with the group.

Language focus 2

was/were: questions

1 ★ **Complete the questions and short answers in the grammar table.**

1	**A:** _____ you at the concert last night?
	B: Yes, I _____ .
2	**A:** _____ the bands good?
	B: No, they _____ .

2 ★★ **Put the words in order to make questions. Then write the answers. You can check your answers on page 20 of the Student's Book.**

1 Columbus / born / was / Where / ?
Where was Columbus born? In ___Genoa___ .

2 Anne Frank / during / was / the Second World War / Where?
_____ In _____ .

3 Tim Berners-Lee's / What / job / was?
_____ He _____

4 family / Anne Frank / and / Who / of / were / her / afraid?
_____ They _____

5 was / Columbus / 1492 / Where / in?
_____ In _____

6 the / What / of / Tim Berners-Lee's / name / was / invention?
_____ The _____

Past simple: questions

3 ★★ **Complete the questions to a teenager who sailed across the Atlantic alone. Use the question words and words in brackets to help you.**

How long   How many   What   ~~When~~   Where

1 *When did you decide* to sail across the Atlantic? (you/ decide)
Last year.

2 _____ ? (the trip / take)
Seven weeks.

3 _____ hours _____ at night? (you / sleep)
Two or three.

4 _____ a lot of sharks? (you / see)
Yes, and dolphins.

5 _____ all day? (you / do)
I looked after the boat.

6 _____ the trip? (you / finish)
In the Caribbean.

4 ★★★ **Write questions in the past simple about the underlined information.**

1 Marie Curie won the Nobel Prize for Physics in 1903.
What did Marie Curie win in 1903?

2 Christopher Columbus made his fourth and final voyage in 1502.
_____

3 Anne Frank and her family lived in those small rooms for two years.
_____

4 Tim Berners-Lee studied at Oxford from 1973 to 1976.
_____

5 Marie Curie was born in Poland in 1867.
_____

6 The USA made Columbus Day a holiday in 1937.
_____

5 ★★★ **Imagine you are interviewing Tim Berners-Lee. Read the answers and write the correct questions.**

1 *Where were you born?*
I was born in England.

2 _____
I studied Engineering at Oxford University.

3 _____
I called it the *World Wide Web* because I knew it was for the whole world.

4 _____
Oh, yes I made lots of mistakes – like the '//' in web addresses. It's really not necessary!

Explore the suffix -ness

6 ★ **Circle the adjectives in the box that do not add -ness to make a noun.**

sad   favourite   tidy   kind   funny
~~ill~~   brilliant   happy   big   weak

7 ★★ **Complete the sentences with words from Exercise 6.**

1 His uncle has a very serious ___illness___ .

2 My teacher really likes the _____ of my homework.

3 Thank you very much for your _____ .

4 Brendan felt a great _____ when his cat died.

5 Liam's very good at football – his only _____ is his left foot.

6 My grandmother always said that _____ was the most important thing in life.

Reading

The Heroes of BRITAIN

Every autumn a TV channel organises the Pride of Britain awards ceremony. The awards **celebrate** people who make the world a better place and **inspire** others. The winners are ordinary people, but they all did something extraordinary. The programme shows a special film about each winner. They are children, teenagers and adults, from six to 95 years old. The public, charities and the emergency services (firefighters, police, etc.) send in the names of people they want to win, and famous actors, politicians and singers present the awards.

Here are some recent winners:

Child of Courage:
TOM PHILLIPS, 9

When a bull attacked Tom's dad on their farm, Tom drove the farm **tractor** (for the first time!) at the bull and saved his dad's life.

Teenager of Courage:
JACK CARROLL, 14

Jack has cerebral palsy and needs a **wheelchair**, but he still hopes to become a professional comedian. He first **performed** at a party for his parents, and then posted the video on YouTube. He often makes jokes about his **disability**.

Great Bravery:
LUCY GALE, 33

Lucy, a taxi driver, saved two drivers after their cars crashed on a train crossing. She then moved one of the cars off the crossing seconds before an express train passed, and stopped a terrible train crash.

1 ★ **Read the text about a special TV programme. Tick (✓) the kind of people in the programme.**

actors and singers	☐	sportspeople	☐
children	✓	brave people	☐
teenagers	☐	heroes	☐

2 ★ **Look at the words in bold in the text. What kind of words (noun or verb) are they?**
1 celebrate ___verb___
2 inspire _____
3 tractor _____
4 wheelchair _____
5 performed _____
6 disability _____

3 ★★ **Complete the definitions with the correct form of the words from Exercise 2.**
1 A person who can't walk needs a _wheelchair_ .
2 A _____ is a large form of transport we use on a farm.
3 A _____ is an illness or injury that makes it difficult to do things other people can do.
4 Sometimes you want to do something because someone _____ you to do it.
5 When we say we admire someone and show them how much we like them, we _____ them.
6 When someone _____ , they tell other people stories or jokes, dance or play a musical instrument for them.

4 ★★ **Read the text again. Circle the correct answer for each question.**
1 When can you see the *Pride of Britain* awards ceremony?
   a once a year   **b** every four years
   c in the summer
2 What type of people win awards?
   a famous actors   **b** people who helped others
   c politicians
3 Who doesn't send in names of people to win the awards?
   a the public   **b** singers
   c police or ambulance workers
4 Who saved two people?
   a Tom   **b** Jack   **c** Lucy
5 Who doesn't usually use anything with wheels?
   a Tom   **b** Jack   **c** Lucy
6 Who wants to be famous one day?
   a Tom   **b** Jack   **c** Lucy

5 ★★★ **Is there an award like the *Pride of Britain* in your country? Do you know about anyone who is an 'ordinary' hero? What did they do?**

Writing

A description of a person you admire

1 Read Patrick's description of a person he admires. Why was Judith by the river?

One person I admire is Judith, a girl who lives on my street. She's older than I am but she's in my sister's class and they're in the same swimming club as well.

She's got a dog so she often takes it for walks by the river at the back of our house. Last winter a small boy fell into the river and couldn't swim. Judith heard him scream and didn't stop to think. Although the water was very cold, she jumped in to rescue him. The boy disappeared under the water, but Judith stayed calm and pulled him out. A neighbour saw them and went to help them get out of the water. They were both fine after they got warm again.

I admire her because she saved the boy's life, but she says it was nothing special! She is very brave. The boy's parents think she is a hero and I agree.

2 Read the description again. Answer the questions.
1. How does Patrick know Judith? _____
2. Why did the boy scream? _____
3. What did Judith do? _____
4. What happened when they were in the water? _____
5. What does Judith think about what happened? _____

Connectors ———————

3 Look back at the text. Which words does Patrick use to join these ideas? Where do they go in the sentence?
1. My sister and Judith are in the same class. They are in the same swimming club.
   and (in the middle), as well (at the end)
2. She's got a dog. She often takes it for walks by the river.
   _____
3. The water was very cold. She jumped in to rescue him.
   _____
4. I admire her. She saved the boy's life.
   _____

4 Join the sentences using the connectors in brackets.
1. The bag was very heavy. He carried it for her. (although)
   Although the bag was very heavy, he carried it for her.
2. We live in the same street. We go to the same school. (and, as well)
   _____
3. We both like music. We decided to start a band together. (so)
   _____
4. The man couldn't get up the stairs. He was in a wheelchair. (because)
   _____

5 Look back at the text. Find apostrophes and match them with their uses.
1. ___*She's*___ = She is
2. _____ = possession
3. _____ = they are
4. _____ = could not
5. _____ = She has

6 Write apostrophes in the correct place in the sentences.
1. They͵re my sister͵s best friends.
2. Shes a real hero because she saved the boys life.
3. Were in the same class so were the same age.
4. Life wasnt easy for her and she didnt have a lot of money.
5. Id like to be like him when Im older.

Writing

> **WRITING TIP**
> Make it better! ✓ ✓ ✓
> Use the infinitive with *to* to explain the purpose of an action (why someone did something).
> *I went to the shop to buy some bread.*

7 **Complete the sentences with the infinitive form of the verbs in the box.**

> make   become   rescue   ~~help~~   find out   earn

1 She heard a girl shout so she ran ___*to help*___ her.
2 We called our friend _____ what happened.
3 He studied very hard _____ a doctor.
4 They worked very hard _____ enough money.
5 He climbed the tree _____ the cat.
6 Gary went slowly _____ sure he didn't fall.

> **WRITING TIP**
> Make it better! ✓ ✓ ✓
> Write about the person's character – use adjectives to say what the person is like.
> *My aunt can be quite serious but she's very kind, too.*

8 **Read the sentences. Which one does <u>not</u> describe someone's character?**

1 She's really friendly and she talks to everyone.
2 Linda is kind and always finds time for her friends.
3 My uncle is very brave but he doesn't think so.
4 He's quite young and he's tall and strong.
5 Robbie always tells jokes – he's really funny.

9 **Look back at Patrick's description. Order the things he talks about.**

> what other people think of him/her
> ~~who the person is~~   why you admire them
> how you know the person   what the person did
> the person's character

1 *who the person is* _____
2 _____
3 _____
4 _____
5 _____
6 _____

PLAN

10 **Choose a person you know and admire to write about. Use the things in Exercise 9 and make notes.**

WRITE

11 **Write the description. Look at page 27 of the Student's Book to help you.**

_____
_____
_____
_____
_____
_____
_____
_____
_____
_____
_____
_____
_____

CHECK

12 **Check your writing. Can you say YES to these questions?**

- Is the information from Exercise 9 in your description?
- Do you describe the person's character and say why you admire them?
- Do you use connectors to join sentences?
- Do you use the infinitive with *to* to explain the purpose?
- Do you use apostrophes correctly?
- Are the spelling and punctuation correct?

Do you need to write a second draft?

Vocabulary

Jobs

1 Match the words in the box with the jobs in the pictures.

| dancer   police officer   musician   actor   nurse   artist   vet   ~~astronaut~~   scientist   firefighter |

1 _astronaut_

2 _____

3 _____

4 _____

5 _____

6 _____

7 _____

8 _____

9 _____

10 _____

Total: 9

Adjectives of character

2 Circle the correct words.

1 I don't like going to the dentist. I'm not very **brave** / friendly.

2 Ellen usually laughs and smiles all day. She's very **funny** / **cheerful**.

3 Steven doesn't like talking. He's very **calm** / **quiet**.

4 Jessie always helps me with my homework. He's very **kind** / **stubborn**.

5 Jenny isn't nervous about exams. She's very **calm** / **serious**.

6 Max works hard at school. He's very **serious** / **brave**.

7 His stories always make me laugh. He's very **cheerful** / **funny**.

Total: 6

Language focus

was/were and past simple: affirmative and negative

3 Complete the sentences with the past form of the verbs in brackets.

1 I ___was___ born in Switzerland and I _____ to school in France. (be, go)

2 Bill _____ Science but he _____ good at languages. (study, not be)

3 Jane _____ around the world and _____ a book about her journey. (sail, write)

4 Maria _____ music but she _____ a famous singer. (not study, become)

5 Danny _____ good at art, but he _____ to be an artist. (be, not want)

Total: 9

Past simple: questions

4 Write a question for each answer.

1 **A:** Where / born?
  Where were you born?
  B: I was born in Italy.

2 **A:** What / study?
  _____
  B: She studied Geography.

3 **A:** / good at sport?
  _____
  B: No, they weren't good at sport.

4 **A:** / play tennis at school?
  _____
  B: Yes, we did.

5 **A:** What / your book about?
  _____
  B: My book was about mountain climbing.

Total: 4

Language builder

5 Choose the correct options.

Cheryl:	What ¹_____ yesterday? ²_____ you busy?
Jake:	I ³_____ in the music shop on Saturday mornings. It ⁴_____ really busy on Saturdays.
Cheryl:	Do you like ⁵_____ there?
Jake:	Yes, I ⁶_____. But yesterday I ⁷_____ up late and then I ⁸_____ late for work.
Cheryl:	Oh no!
Jake:	The manager ⁹_____ very happy!
Cheryl:	Do you play ¹⁰_____ musical instruments?
Jake:	Yes, I ¹¹_____ to play the guitar.

1 **a** are you doing   **ⓑ** did you do
2 **a** Was   **b** Were
3 **a** work   **b** works
4 **a** is usually   **b** usually is
5 **a** work   **b** working
6 **a** am   **b** do
7 **a** got   **b** get
8 **a** am   **b** was
9 **a** wasn't   **b** weren't
10 **a** any   **b** much
11 **a** learn   **b** 'm learning

Total: 10

Vocabulary builder

6 Choose the correct options.

1 You can sometimes _____ extra pocket money by washing cars.
   ⓐ earn   **b** spend   **c** borrow
2 A _____ studies Chemistry, Physics, or Biology.
   a scientist   **b** dancer   **c** writer
3 You can usually buy magazines in _____ .
   a a shoe shop **b** a newsagent
   c a clothes shop
4 Bill isn't scared. He's very _____ .
   a serious   **b** cheerful   **c** brave
5 I'm trying to _____ money by not buying chocolate.
   a spend   **b** save   **c** earn
6 _____ creates pictures and paintings.
   a An actor   **b** An artist
   c An astronaut
7 Nina helps other people. She is very _____ .
   a serious   **b** quiet   **c** kind
8 You can buy medicine in _____ .
   a an electronics shop **b** a sports shop
   c a chemist

Total: 7

Speaking

7 Complete the conversation with the words in the box.

look   may   That   ~~think~~   maybe   sure

Luke:	Who do you ¹_*think*_ it is?
Oli:	I'm not ²_____ . He ³_____ be a footballer.
Luke:	No, he doesn't ⁴_____ very sporty.
Oli:	OK, then ⁵_____ he's a singer.
Luke:	⁶_____ 's possible.

Total: 5

Total: 50

was/were

1 Complete the text with *was* or *were*.

Yesterday, my mum [1] _was_ at the shopping mall all afternoon. My dad and my brother [2] _____ at a football match. So I [3] _____ at home alone. I watched a couple of programmes on TV, but they [4] _____ boring. I texted my friends, Anna and Maria, but they [5] _____ both busy. I started my homework, but it [6] _____ too difficult.

Spell it right! Shopping words

Remember to spell these clothes and shopping words correctly.

shopping	~~shoping~~	trainers	~~trainners~~
bought	~~bougth~~	trousers	~~trausers~~
expensive	~~spensive~~	T-shirt	~~T-shir~~

was/were: questions

Remember that:

- we make questions with **was/were** before the subject.
  - ✓ **Were you** at home last night?
  - ✗ ~~You were at home last night?~~
- we make information questions with the *Wh-* question word + **was/were** + subject.
  - ✓ **Where were you** last night?
  - ✗ ~~Where you were last night?~~
- we make questions with *how many* + subject + **was/were**.
  - ✓ **How many students were** in your class?
  - ✗ ~~How many were students in your class?~~

2 Read the sentences about a party. Write the correct questions. Use *was/were*.

1 I was at a party on Saturday night.
   Where were you on Saturday night ?

2 The party was at Mary's house.
   _____ ?

3 No, I wasn't late. I arrived at 8 o'clock.
   _____ ?

4 There were 20 people at the party.
   _____ ?

5 Yes, Peter and his brother were at the party.
   _____ ?

6 I was at the party for three hours.
   _____ ?

7 Yes, all the people at the party were happy.
   _____ ?

Jobs

Remember that:

- we use *a* or *an* to talk about a person who does a particular job.
  - ✓ *My brother wants to be **a** firefighter.*
  - ✗ ~~My brother wants to be firefighter.~~
- we use *a* before consonants and **an** before vowel sounds.

3 Read the text. Add *a* or *an* in the correct places.

My friend James has got two brothers. Their dad is ^*a* famous artist and their mum is vet. But the brothers don't want to be artists or vets. James wants to be actor because he loves the theatre. His brother, Paul, would like to be firefighter or astronaut, but he isn't tall enough, so he wants to be police officer. And his younger brother, Michael, loves music, but he can't be singer, because he can't sing. But he plays the piano very well, so, maybe he will be musician.

Expressions with *make*

Remember, some nouns have **make** before them, but other nouns have **do** before them.

- ✓ *I want to **make a cake** for my sister's birthday.*
- ✗ ~~I want to do a cake for my sister's birthday.~~
- ✓ *Police officers make sure people don't **do bad things**.*
- ✗ ~~Police officers make sure people don't make bad things.~~

4 Complete the sentences with *make* or *do*.

1 Arturo didn't _____do_____ his homework yesterday.

2 I'd like to _____ a suggestion.

3 What job do you want to _____ when you leave school?

4 What sports do you _____ in your free time?

5 I want to _____ friends with new people from different countries.

6 They like speaking English, but they often _____ mistakes.

7 Sara is ill, so she can't _____ the exam.

8 She works hard and helps people because she wants to _____ a difference.

③ Strange stories

Vocabulary

Action verbs

1 ★ **Find seven more action verbs in the word search. Write them under the correct picture.**

t	h	r	o	w	o	s	f	h	e
f	a	l	l	o	v	e	r	i	g
c	h	a	u	c	o	r	c	d	k
a	k	t	j	e	s	g	h	e	p
t	p	r	u	n	a	w	a	y	s
c	l	i	m	b	m	t	s	e	c
h	e	i	p	o	n	e	e	i	o
g	e	t	y	o	p	l	h	s	c

1 _throw_

2 _____

3 _____

4 _____

5 _____

6 _____

7 _____

8 _____

2 ★★ **Complete the sentences with the past simple form of the verbs from Exercise 1.**

1 He ___*threw*___ the empty bottle in the bin.
2 I didn't see the bag on the floor so I _____ it.
3 They _____ their friend across the park.
4 The police _____ the thieves at the airport with all the money.
5 My sister _____ Mont Blanc last summer. It's 4,810m high!
6 When I saw the big dog, I _____ . It was enormous!
7 The thief _____ out of the window.
8 My little brother _____ my mobile phone under the sofa for a joke. It wasn't funny.

3 ★★★ **Complete the story with the correct form of the words in Exercise 1.**

> Why did my English teacher ¹___*chase*___ me around the school? There was no time to think. 'You can't ²_____ me,' I said! I ³_____ out of the window into the playground and ⁴_____ away. I tried to jump over the PE teacher's bicycle but it was too high and I ⁵_____ over and hurt my leg. I got up quickly, went to the car park and ⁶_____ behind the French teacher's car. The English teacher ⁷_____ on to the car next me and ⁸_____ his books at me. He was shouting my name: 'Justin! Justin!' Then I woke up … in my English class. The teacher smiled at me and said, 'You fell asleep, Justin!'

4 ★★★ **Write five sentences with the verbs in Exercise 1 about you or someone you know.**

When I was six, I fell over some books in my bedroom.

_____

_____

_____

_____

_____

Language focus 1

Past continuous

1 ★ Complete the table.

	I / he / she / it	you / we / they
+	I [1] _was_ running away.	We [6] _____ hiding.
-	He [2] _____ running away.	They [7] _____ hiding.
?	[3] _____ she running away? Yes, she [4] _____ . No, she [5] _____ .	[8] _____ they hiding? Yes, they [9] _____ . No, they [10] _____ .

2 ★★ Look at the picture and write sentences.

When the object appeared in the sky …

1 … we / play / football in the garden
We were playing football in the garden.

2 … my friend / catch / a ball
_____

3 … my sister / climb / a tree
_____

4 … my mum / talk / to a friend on the phone
_____

5 … a car / drive / down the street
_____

6 … our dog / chase / the car
_____

7 … my neighbour / cut / the grass
_____

8 … the police officers / help / an old lady
_____

Past continuous questions

3 ★★ Complete the detective's questions with the words in the box and the past continuous. Then complete the short answers.

> the men / carry   you and your friends / play
> ~~the woman / wear~~   you / watch   the man / drive

1 _Was the woman wearing_ glasses?
No, _she wasn't_ .

2 _____ TV at nine o'clock?
Yes, _____ .

3 _____ a big box?
No, _____ .

4 _____ the car?
No, _____ . It was the woman.

5 _____ football?
Yes, _____ . In the park.

4 ★★★ Write questions with the past continuous. Answer them for you.

1 What / you / wear / yesterday?
What were you wearing yesterday?
I was wearing a red T-shirt and black jeans.

2 What / you / do / at eight o'clock / this morning?
_____
_____

3 Who / you / talk to / on the phone / all afternoon?
_____
_____

4 you / listen to music / an hour ago?
_____
_____

Explore expressions with *look*

5 ★★ Match the sentence beginnings (1–5) with the sentence endings (a–e).

1 Tom was looking after his little brother   _c_
2 I was looking in the kitchen window   ___
3 Lydia was looking for her mobile phone   ___
4 We were looking at some photos   ___
5 Some people say I look like my mum   ___

a when we saw something really funny.
b when I saw my mum drop the cake.
c because his parents were at work.
d but other people say I look like my dad.
e when she found some money.

Listening and vocabulary

Adverbs of manner

1 ★ **Write the adverbs for the adjectives below.**
1 careful __carefully__
2 easy _____
3 good _____
4 happy _____
5 quick _____
6 quiet _____
7 bad _____
8 slow _____

2 ★★ **Complete the sentences with the adverbs from Exercise 1.**
1 The weather is bad so drive ____slowly____ .
2 We played very _____ so the other team won.
3 He saw a big elephant so he ran away _____ .
4 The mountain was very high so we walked up it _____ .
5 I did _____ in my exam because I studied a lot.
6 We spoke _____ so nobody could hear us.
7 I was listening to music quite _____ until I remembered my homework!
8 It wasn't a high wall so we climbed over it _____ .

3 ★★★ **Complete the sentences with the adverbs from Exercise 1.**
1 It wasn't difficult to pass the exam.
I passed the exam ____easily____ .
2 We didn't drive fast.
We drove _____ .
3 We weren't being noisy.
We were talking very _____ .
4 I'm not very good at playing the guitar.
I play the guitar _____ .
5 He wasn't sad when he was singing.
He was singing _____ .
6 They are very good at volleyball.
They play volleyball very _____ .

Listening

4 ★ 🔊 **03** **Listen to Vicky talking to her friend Mel about a book. What kind of book is it?** (Circle) **the correct option.**
a an adventure book
b a travel book
c a science-fiction story

5 ★★ 🔊 **03** **Listen again and choose the correct answers.**
1 Vicky said sorry because …
   a she was late.
   (b) she didn't go to Mel's house yesterday.
2 The name of the book was …
   a *The Thief Lord*.
   b *Cornelia Funke*.
3 It was a good book so Vicky …
   a was reading until six o'clock.
   b didn't stop until the end.
4 Prosper and Bo ran away …
   a to stay together.
   b to find their mother.
5 They went to Venice because …
   a it was their mother's favourite place.
   b they knew some children there.
6 The Thief Lord took things from …
   a Barbarossa.
   b people with a lot of money.
7 Vicky says she liked the story because it was …
   a surprising.
   b magical.
8 Vicky doesn't tell Mel the end of the story because …
   a it's very complicated.
   b she wants Mel to read the book.

Language focus 2

Past simple vs. continuous

1 ★ **Match the parts of the sentences to make rules.**

1 We use the past simple
2 We use the past continuous
a to talk about an action that was in progress in the past.
b to talk about a short, finished action in the past.

2 ★★ Circle **the correct options in the story.**

An Italian man ¹ **looked /** was looking at a painting on the wall in his father's kitchen. The painting looked like something he once ² **saw / was seeing** in a book about the famous French painter Paul Gauguin. His father ³ **told / was telling** him he found the painting many years ago on a train when he ⁴ **travelled / was travelling** to Paris. His son read about the painting on the Internet and ⁵ **found out / was finding out** that it was really a painting by Gauguin. The police discovered the interesting story behind the painting. A man ⁶ **went / was going to** an old lady's house to clean the windows. While the old lady ⁷ **made / was making** some tea, the man took the painting off the wall and ⁸ **left / was leaving** the house quietly. While he ⁹ **sat / was sitting** on the train, he realised he ¹⁰ **didn't know / wasn't knowing** what to do with the painting so he left it carefully on the seat.

could(n't)

3 ★ **Complete the sentences with the words in the box.**

> could   past   couldn't   subject

1 We use *could* and *couldn't* + infinitive without *to* to talk about ability in the _____ .
2 Questions: *Could* + _____ + infinitive?
3 Short answers: Yes, she _____ . No, they _____ .

4 ★★ **Complete the conversation with *could* or *couldn't*.**

A: What's the Loch Ness monster?
B: Well, in Scotland there's a lake called Loch Ness. They say a monster lives in the lake but nobody ¹ _could_ find it.
A: Why do they think there's a monster in the lake?
B: Well, someone took a photo in 1937. In the photo you ² _____ see a long neck and a head above the water. And there's a video from 2007 as well. A man said he ³ _____ see something long and black in the water but he ⁴ _____ see what it was. Scientists spent many years looking in the lake but they ⁵ _____ find anything.
A: Are there any other photos of it?
B: Well, a man was looking at maps on his computer in 2014 and said he ⁶ _____ see something in a photo of the lake.
A: I'd like to go there.
B: You ⁷ _____ go there because it's in Scotland and you hate the cold!

Past simple, past continuous and *could*

5 ★★★ **Read the conversation and write questions with the past simple, past continuous or *could*.**

Policeman:	¹ *What were you doing when you saw the light?*
Man:	I was driving.
Policeman:	² _____
Man:	Because I was going home.
Policeman:	³ _____
Man:	Well, I couldn't see much, only a very big object and bright lights.
Policeman:	⁴ _____
Man:	No, I didn't see anyone else.

Explore nouns with -er

6 ★★ **Write the names of the people with –er.**

1 I live on an island.   *islander*
2 I take photos. _____
3 I work on a farm. _____
4 I explore new places. _____
5 I build things. _____
6 I'm shopping. _____
7 I'm swimming. _____
8 I paint. _____

Reading

1 ★ **Read the article. What was in the water?**

A plane CRASH?

In March 2014, islanders on Gran Canaria were looking at the sea when they saw a big yellow object. It was long, with a yellow tail and it was in the water near the **coast**. They called the emergency services – the police, ambulances and the coast guard.

The emergency services told the newspapers that a plane was in the Atlantic Ocean about one kilometre from the coast of Gran Canaria.

At about 3 pm, the BBC and other TV channels around the world began to **report** that a Boeing 737 **crashed** into the sea. Workers in the **control tower** at the airport in Gran Canaria **confirmed** the reports: 'We are missing a plane!' one airport worker said. Another plane that was flying over the area also saw the plane in the water.

A helicopter and a boat went out to sea to rescue the passengers but when they arrived, they found nothing. There was only a large tugboat – a boat that pulls other boats across the sea.

Finally, the emergency services confirmed the **false alarm**. It was not a plane – just a boat that looked a bit like a plane. Nobody knows what happened to the 'missing plane' from the airport!

2 ★★ **Match the words in bold with the definitions.**

1 A building at an airport where they watch planes.   *control tower*
2 To say that something was definitely true.   _____
3 The land near the sea.   _____
4 When someone thinks something is going to happen but it doesn't.   _____
5 Give information about something.   _____
6 When a car, plane or train hits something else.   _____

3 ★★★ **Read the text again and put the events in the correct order.**

a They found a tugboat.   ___
b They called the emergency services.   ___
c A helicopter and a boat went to the plane.   ___
d TV channels said a plane was in the sea.   ___
e People saw a plane in the sea.   _1_
f Airport workers said a plane was missing.   ___

4 ★★★ **Do you know any stories about false alarms? Can you invent one? Write five sentences.**

_____
_____
_____
_____
_____

Writing

A story

1 Read the story. What did Mr James do?

One day last year, a homeless man, Glen James, found a bag in the door of a shop while he was walking around a shopping centre in Boston.

At first, he didn't know what to do, but when he opened the bag he saw it had $40,000 in it so then he took it to the police. Many people thought that Mr James did a wonderful thing. Later, a website decided to raise money to help Mr James because he had no home or job. Finally, they raised over $140,000 from people all over the world. Mr James said 'I'm really surprised and so happy. This is going to change my life.'

2 Read the story again. Answer the questions.

1 What was Glen James doing when he found the bag? _____
2 What was in the bag? _____
3 Who did Mr James give the bag to? _____
4 How much did the website raise for Mr James? _____

Useful language Sequencing language 1 _____

3 Look back at the story. Find sequencing words and phrases.

1 O _ne day_ _____
2 w_____
3 A__ f_____
4 w_____
5 t_____
6 L_____
7 F_____

4 Complete the story with the words and phrases from Exercise 3.

¹ _One day_ last summer a woman was walking in the park ² _____ she found a lost dog. ³ _____ , she didn't know what to do because she had a sick child. She didn't think she could look after a dog and a child, so she put a poster up in her village, but nobody came to collect the dog. ⁴ _____ , one afternoon ⁵ _____ she was working in her garden, the dog started to make lots of noise. She followed it into the kitchen and found her son on the floor. ⁶ _____ , the doctors said her son almost died but the dog saved him before it was too late. ⁷ _____ , the woman decided to keep the dog because it saved her son's life.

5 Be careful with the spelling of the past simple. Write the past simple forms of these verbs.

1 go   _went_   6 try   _____
2 be   _____   7 drive _____
       _____   8 give   _____
3 have _____   9 find   _____
4 get   _____   10 catch _____
5 buy   _____

Writing

> **WRITING TIP**
> Make it better! ✓ ✓ ✓
> Describe your (or the other person's) reaction or feeling when something happens.
> *I was really surprised when I heard the news about Grandma.*

6 Complete the sentences with the words in the box.

> sad   frightened   happy   angry   ~~surprised~~

1 When I saw the huge present, I was very __surprised__ .
2 He's _____ because his brother broke his new tablet.
3 When my cat died, I felt really _____ .
4 I was really _____ because, finally, I found my mobile phone.
5 When he saw the snake, he was very _____ .

7 Read the story in Exercise 4 again and make notes about the information in the table.

when the story happened	*last year*
where the story happened	
people in the story	
what they were doing	
events of the story	
how the story ended	
the people's feelings in the story	

PLAN

8 Read the titles for a story below and choose one you like. Use the table in Exercise 7 and make notes. You can use your imagination or write about a true story.

A mysterious incident

A mysterious object

A mysterious person

WRITE

9 Write the story. Look at page 39 of the Student's Book to help you.

_____
_____
_____
_____
_____
_____
_____
_____
_____
_____
_____

CHECK

10 Check your writing. Can you say YES to these questions?
- Is the information from Exercise 9 in your description?
- Do you describe your/the person's reaction or feelings?
- Do you use sequencing words to order the events in the story?
- Do you spell the past simple forms correctly?

Do you need to write a second draft?

Vocabulary
Action verbs

1 Circle the correct options.
1 The thief jumped / threw out of the window.
2 The burglars hid / climbed over a wall.
3 A neighbour ran / chased the thief into the garden.
4 The thief fell over / threw and broke her arm.
5 He caught / hid the money in a tree.
6 He threw / chased the newspaper in the bin.

Total: 5

Adverbs of manner

2 Put the letters in order to make adjectives. Change them to adverbs to complete each sentence.
1 I looked __carefully__ for my keys. (farlecu)
2 It was cold so I walked home _____ . (kuqic)
3 We found the address _____ . (saye)
4 We lost because we weren't playing _____ . (ogdo)
5 The baby is sleeping, so please talk _____ . (tiqeu)
6 It's Sam's birthday and he is singing _____ . (pypah)
7 Tina was very tired so she cycled _____ . (oswl)
8 I did very _____ in the exam. My parents were angry. (dba)

Total: 7

Language focus
Past continuous

3 Complete the interview with the correct form of the past continuous.

Detective:	¹ __Were__ you __watching__ (watch) from the window?
Peter:	Yes, I ² _____ .
Detective:	What ³ _____ the men _____ (wear)?
Peter:	One man ⁴ _____ (wear) a brown jacket.
Detective:	⁵ _____ he _____ (carry) anything?
Peter:	Yes, he ⁶ _____ (carry) a black bag.
Detective:	⁷ _____ the men _____ (run)?
Peter:	No, they ⁸ _____ , but they ⁹ _____ (walk) quickly.

Total: 8

Past simple vs. past continuous

4 Circle the correct options.
1 We ate / were eating dinner when the lights went / were going off.
2 We slept / were sleeping when the thieves broke / were breaking into the house.
3 One thief fell / was falling over while he ran / was running away.
4 The police found / were finding the money while they searched / were searching the garden.
5 One thief drove / was driving away in a car while the police didn't look / weren't looking.

Total: 9

could(n't)

5 Look at the pictures of Tom and complete the sentences with *could* or *couldn't* and the correct verb.

When Tom was five, he ¹ __could read__ stories, but he ² _____ . He ³ _____ a bike without any problems and he was very musical so he ⁴ _____ the guitar very well when he was ten, but he ⁵ _____ the piano. Now he's 14 and he can do all of these things. What about you?

Total: 4

Vocabulary builder

6 (Circle) the correct words.

1 After school, Danny _____ judo.
   a goes   **(b)** does   **c** plays

2 I'm _____ because I want to buy a new phone.
   a saving   **b** selling   **c** spending

3 I sometimes buy this magazine at the _____.
   a chemist   **b** shoe shop   **c** newsagent

4 Larry talks to everybody. He's very _____.
   a calm   **b** kind   **c** friendly.

5 I love animals so I'd like to be a _____.
   a vet   **b** actor   **c** nurse

6 A man _____ over the wall into our garden.
   a chased   **b** climbed   **c** caught

7 I did my homework _____ so I didn't make mistakes.
   a carefully   **b** easily   **c** badly

8 He's got three cameras. He looks _____ a photographer.
   a for   **b** after   **c** like

9 When he saw the police officers, he _____ so they couldn't find him.
   a threw   **b** hid   **c** fell over

10 I _____ listening to music in my room last night.
   a were   **b** was   **c** am

Total: 9

Language builder

7 (Circle) the correct words.

Kim: [1]_____ you watch the detective show on TV last night? It [2]_____ really good!

Bill: No, I [3]_____ my homework. I [4]_____ a test this morning. But I love detective shows. What [5]_____ it about?

Kim: A group of thieves stole [6]_____ diamonds and the police [7]_____ understand how they did it.

Bill: What [8]_____ in the end?

Kim: I don't know. The final episode is on this evening. Do you want to watch it together?

Bill: OK!

1 **a** Do   **(b)** Did   **c** Were
2 **a** was   **b** were   **c** did
3 **a** did   **b** was doing   **c** am doing
4 **a** was having   **b** was   **c** had
5 **a** were   **b** was   **c** did
6 **a** much   **b** any   **c** some
7 **a** weren't   **b** couldn't   **c** aren't
8 **a** happened   **b** happen   **c** was happening

Total: 7

Speaking

8 **Complete the conversation with the words in the box.**

next   do   ~~strange~~   weird   did   What

A: Something [1] *strange* happened yesterday.
B: Really? [2]_____ ?
A: Well, I was walking home through the park.
B: What happened [3]_____ ?
A: I fell over but I don't know how it happened. And then a boy was standing next to me and he helped me to stand up.
B: What [4]_____ you say?
A: Well, I said thanks, of course.
B: What did you [5]_____ ?
A: I picked up my bag and when I stood up, the boy was gone. There was nobody in the park.
B: That's [6]_____ !

Total: 5

Total: 54

Get it right! Unit 3

Past simple vs. past continuous

Remember that:

- we use **was** or **were** + **-ing** to talk about an action that was in progress in the past.
  - ✓ The dog **was chasing** the cat.
  - ✗ ~~The dog chasing the cat.~~
- we use the past simple to talk about completed events and actions in the past. We never use **was** or **were** + past simple.
  - ✓ The dog **chased** the cat.
  - ✗ ~~The dog was chased the cat.~~
- we usually use **while** with the past continuous and **when** with the past simple.
  - ✓ The dog was chasing the cat **when** the man appeared.
  - ✗ ~~The dog chased the cat while the man was appearing.~~

1 Circle the correct words.

> ✉ **New mail**
>
> Dear Martin,
> We went to the beach last weekend. Three of my cousins [1] **were came / came** with us. And our dog, Charlie, of course! It [2] **rained / was raining** when we left the house, but while we [3] **driving / were driving** there, the rain stopped. At first, everybody [4] **was wanting / wanted** to do different things. My parents wanted to sit and read. My cousins [5] **were decided / decided** to go swimming in the sea. We really [6] **enjoyed / were enjoyed** our day at the beach.
> I hope you had a good weekend, too,
> Jamie

could(n't)

Remember that:

- we use the infinitive without *to* after **could(n't)**.
  - ✓ The test was easy. I **could answer** all the questions.
  - ✗ ~~The test was easy. I could to answer all the questions.~~
- we never use the past simple after **could(n't)**.
  - ✓ They **couldn't open** the door.
  - ✗ ~~They couldn't opened the door.~~
- we use **could(n't)**, not *can('t)*, to talk about ability in the past.
  - ✓ I'm sorry you **couldn't** come to my house yesterday.
  - ✗ ~~I'm sorry you can't come to my house yesterday.~~

2 Are the sentences correct? Correct the incorrect sentences.

1 I can't go to the cinema last night because I was looking after my sister.
   I couldn't go to the cinema last night because I was looking after my sister.

2 I could hear the music but I couldn't see who was playing it.
   _____

3 It was great to see you. I'm so happy that you could to come.
   _____

4 We couldn't went to the beach because it was raining.
   _____

5 In the past, you couldn't to travel from London to Paris by train.
   _____

6 The exam was very difficult. I can't understand the questions.
   _____

Adjectives or adverbs?

Remember that:

- we use an adverb to describe a verb or an action.
  - ✓ He looked **carefully** at the picture.
  - ✗ ~~He looked careful at the picture.~~
- we use an adjective after **be** with an imperative.
  - ✓ **Be careful**! That water is very hot.
  - ✗ ~~Be carefully! That water is very hot.~~

3 Complete the sentences with a word from the box. Change the adjective to an adverb if necessary.

> good   easy   quiet   careful   quick   bad   ~~loud~~

1 There was a woman speaking ___*loudly*___ on her mobile phone.
2 They speak English very _____ because their mother is English.
3 Be _____ ! I'm trying to study.
4 He plays the piano very _____ . It sounds awful!
5 Did you listen _____ to what the teacher said?
6 I did my homework _____ because I wanted to go to the cinema.
7 He climbed the wall _____ because he's very tall.

Vocabulary

Things in the home

1 ★ **Look at the pictures of the things in the home. Write the words in the correct column. Some words can go in more than one column.**

living room	bedroom	bathroom	other rooms
	mirror	*mirror*	

2 ★★ **Complete the sentences with the words from Exercise 1.**

1 Where's my dictionary? It isn't on my ____*desk*____ or on the _____ with the other books.
2 My dad has two _____ on his bed because he says it's comfortable but I only have one.
3 In winter, I always sleep with a big _____ to keep warm.
4 Houses in the UK usually have _____ on the floor.
5 My little sister can't see herself in our bathroom _____ because she's too short.
6 My mum and dad have got a lot of clothes so their _____ is full.
7 Can you get the sugar? It's in the _____ in the kitchen.
8 When I wake up in the morning, I open the _____ and look outside.

3 ★★★ **Mark and Jane are in their new house but it's empty. Read the sentences and write what they need to buy.**

1 'We haven't got anywhere to put our clothes!'   *wardrobe*
2 'There's nothing on the floor and it's very cold.'   _____
3 'We've got plates and glasses for the kitchen but nowhere to put them.'   _____
4 'I just washed my hands but I can't dry them.'   _____
5 'Our neighbours can see us through the windows!'   _____
6 'We've got nothing on the bed.'   _____ , _____
7 'I need a place to work and somewhere to put my books.'   _____ , _____
8 'I can't believe we can't wash the plates and glasses!'   _____

4 ★★★ **What's your favourite room in your home? Why do you like it? What furniture does it have? What other furniture would you like to have? Write at least five sentences.**

My favourite room is my bedroom. I like it because it's a big, sunny room.

Language focus 1

Comparatives and superlatives

1 ★ **Complete the rules in the grammar table.**

-ier   worse   more (x2)   Better   ~~two~~   -er

1	We use comparative adjectives to compare ___two___ or more people, things, etc.
2	To form the comparative of short adjectives (one syllable) we add _____ .
3	To form the comparative of long adjectives (two syllables +) we use _____ before the adjective.
4	When the adjective has two syllables and ends in -y, we remove the -y and add _____ to form the comparative.
5	_____ (good) and _____ (bad) are irregular comparatives.
6	To make the comparative form of an adverb we usually add _____ .

2 ★★ **Write comparative sentences.**

1 The Empire State Building / high / the Eiffel Tower
The Empire State Building is higher than the Eiffel Tower.
2 Buckingham Palace / big / the White House
3 His desk / expensive / all our furniture
4 A bed / comfortable / a sofa
5 The hotel in Santiago / good / the hotel in Buenos Aires
6 Gail's room / tidy / Kerry's

3 ★ **Choose the correct options to complete the grammar table.**

1	To form the superlative of short adjectives (one syllable) we add *-er* / *-est*.
2	To form the superlative of long adjectives (two syllables +) we use *more* / *most* before the adjective.
3	When the adjective has two syllables and ends in -y, we remove the -y and add *-est* / *-iest* to form the superlative.
4	*Best* / *The best* and *worst* / *the worst* are irregular superlatives.

4 ★ **Complete the text with the superlative form of the adjectives in the box.**

big   expensive   ~~rich~~   tall   ugly   unusual

The billionaire Mukesh Ambani is ¹*the richest* man in India. He and his family live in a house called Antilia, in Mumbai, India. Antilia cost one billion dollars! It's ² _____ house in the world – a tower with 27 floors. It's also ³ _____ family home in the world. There are three floors of gardens and it has ⁴ _____ garage in a family house too, with space for 168 cars, all for Mr Ambani's family of six! Antilia is modern, but it isn't beautiful. In fact, many people think it's ⁵ _____ building in Mumbai. I'm not sure about that, but it's probably ⁶ _____ billionaire's house in the world!

5 ★★★ **Write the sentences in the comparative or superlative.**

1 Mount Everest / high / mountain / in the world
Mount Everest is the highest mountain in the world.
2 This pillow / soft / that pillow
3 The library / quiet / place in the school
4 The beach / relaxing / place to go in the summer
5 A holiday in New York / good / a holiday at home
6 My dad's car / small / my mum's car

Explore expressions with *do*

6 ★★ **Match the sentence beginnings (1–6) with the sentence endings (a–f).**

1 Could you do me a favour?   _c_
2 Can I help you with your homework?   ___
3 My dad can't play football with me   ___
4 I didn't go out on Saturday because   ___
5 Paul was really tired last night because   ___
6 We put all the food in the cupboard   ___

a I was doing my homework all day!
b after we did the shopping.
c Could you give me that book on the shelf?
d because he's doing the housework.
e he did sport for three hours.
f I like doing Maths.

Listening and vocabulary

Household appliances

1 ★ **Add vowels to make words for household appliances. Write them under the correct picture.**

> dshwshr frzr rn ~~frdg~~ wshng mchn
> lmp hrdryr ckr htr

1 ___fridge___ 2 _____ 3 _____

4 _____ 5 _____ 6 _____

7 _____ 8 _____ 9 _____

2 ★★ **Match the words from Exercise 1 with the sentences.**

1 You use this when your hair is wet. ___hairdryer___
2 This washes your clothes. _____
3 It keeps food cool and safe to eat. _____
4 It helps you see in the dark. _____
5 You use this when your house is cold. _____
6 It cleans the plates and glasses. _____
7 It makes your clothes look nice. _____
8 You use this to cook your dinner. _____
9 You can leave food in it for a long time. _____

3 ★★★ **Complete the text with the words from Exercise 1.**

The room with the most appliances in our house is the kitchen. I use the [1] ___cooker___ every evening to make dinner.

We also use the [2]_____ once a day to wash our clothes, and the [3]_____ every day to clean the plates.

Of course, we always use the [4]_____ to keep our food cool and fresh. When my mum cooks, she often puts extra food in the [5]_____ . She says it can stay there for months. One thing I never use is the [6]_____. My mum hates this too, so my dad uses it for his shirts and my T-shirts.

Another thing I use every day is the [7]_____ on my desk – it helps me to see my books because my room is quite dark. And when it's cold, I sometimes use the [8]_____ to stay warm! I've got long hair so I also use my [9]_____ every day.

Listening

4 ★ 🔊 04 **Listen to the conversation between Ella and Nick. What are they talking about?**

5 ★★ 🔊 04 **Listen again. Mark the sentences true (T) or false (F).**

1 Ella and Nick are brother and sister.   _T_
2 They went to see three flats.   ___
3 One flat is really old.   ___
4 Both flats had two bathrooms.   ___
5 Ella likes the first flat better.   ___
6 Nick and Ella usually catch the bus to school.   ___
7 Their mum and dad want to plan a new bedroom.   ___
8 Nick isn't sure the flat is big enough.   ___

Language focus 2

must/mustn't, should/shouldn't

1 ★ (Circle) the correct words.

1 We use *must*, *mustn't*, *should* and *shouldn't* + verb / *to* + verb.
2 We use *must* / *mustn't* to talk about obligation.
3 We use *must* / *mustn't* to talk about prohibition.
4 We use *should* and *shouldn't* to give advice / talk about obligation and prohibition.

2 ★ Complete the sentences with *must* or *mustn't* and a verb from the box.

do eat forget ~~keep~~ learn leave put remember

1 We __must keep__ our room tidy.

2 Your brother _____ his homework while he's watching TV.

3 You _____ the plates in the dishwasher after dinner.

4 You _____ your books and papers all over the living room.

5 I _____ to turn off the oven.

6 Jane _____ how to cook more than pizza!

7 You _____ to bring me your dirty clothes.

8 They _____ all the biscuits. That's too much sugar!

3 ★★ Complete the text with *should* or *shouldn't*.

Feng shui is the old Chinese art of organising your home to bring good health and energy. Here are some ideas about how to improve your house:

- In the bedroom you [1]__should__ always clean under the bed so you don't have negative energy. You [2]_____ keep anything there. The bed [3]_____ never be close to the door or under a window.
- In the living room you [4]_____ put a mirror on the wall to give your house more energy, and you [5]_____ have a plant to show love.
- The colour red is good luck, but you [6]_____ have too much of it because it can make people nervous. Finally, you [7]_____ leave space around the things in the house so energy can move around the room.

Do these things and you [8]_____ have any problems!

4 ★★★ Complete the second sentence so it has the same meaning as the first. Use *should*, *shouldn't*, *must* or *mustn't*.

1 It's a good idea for them to try feng shui. They _should try feng shui._

2 It's not a very good idea to do her homework in the kitchen! She _____

3 Our house rule is to wear slippers inside. You _____ .

4 My advice is to put your desk under the window. I think you _____ .

5 Don't touch that because it's very dangerous! You _____ !

5 ★★★ Complete the sentences about your life at home.

1 My parents say I must _be quicker in the bathroom in the morning, because I'm sometimes late for school._

2 My _____ says I mustn't _____

3 I should _____
_____

4 I shouldn't _____
_____

Explore verbs with *up* or *down*

6 ★★ Complete the sentences with the correct form of the verbs in the box and *up* or *down*.

go lie come (x2) put

1 Why did you climb that wall? You should _come down_ now.

2 Oh no, it's raining. Can you _____ the umbrella?

3 We woke up early and watched the sun _____ .

4 You look tired. Why don't you go and _____ on your bed?

5 The shops are near here. _____ to the top of the road and turn left.

Reading

1 ★ **Read the texts and match the people with the houses in the pictures.**

1 _____

2 _____

3 _____

2 ★★ **Match the words in bold in the text with the definitions.**

1 It's a game where some people hide while one person counts to 100. That person then tries to find everyone. *hide and seek*
2 The same shape as a ball or a circle. _____
3 The part of a room above your head. _____
4 A windmill usually has four of these and they move in the wind. _____
5 To make something full or put things in an empty space. _____
6 Chairs, tables, bed, etc. _____

An unusual place to live

Joey
I live in a windmill! It has five floors and a lot of stairs. The kitchen is at the bottom, the living room is on the first floor, and my bedroom is at the top. It's noisy because of the **sails** in the wind, especially in the winter, but the strangest thing is that the rooms are **round**. Mine is the smallest. It's really difficult to find space for all my things. It's fun here though, and the view is amazing!

Abigail
My friends are always surprised that I live in a 300-year-old house! When my parents bought our house, it was a mess, but now it's beautiful. There are 80 large rooms and 40 bedrooms, so we need a lot of **furniture** to **fill** it. It's a great place for parties, and playing **hide and seek**, but it's easy to get lost!

David
My home is a traditional cottage in a country village. I live here with my parents and my two sisters. It's prettier than my friends' houses, but it's very old, so all the rooms are small and uncomfortable, and the **ceilings** are low. Also, there's only one bathroom, but my parents love it! My room is in the attic. It's very small, and the floor is not very straight. There's only a bed, a cupboard and a small desk under the window.

3 ★★ **Read the text again. Which house is each sentence about? Write *Joey*, *Abigail* or *David*.**

1 The house has a lot of different floors. *Joey*
2 It's good for games. _____
3 It's a strange shape. _____
4 Visitors can choose a room to sleep in. _____
5 It's not good for a big family. _____
6 It isn't quiet. _____
7 Tall people can't live in a house like this. _____
8 It wasn't always a nice house. _____

4 ★★★ **Which of these houses would you like to live in? Why? Do you think your family would like it too? Why/Why not? Write at least five sentences.**

_____
_____
_____
_____
_____

Writing

A description of a house

1 Read Corrine's email about an unusual house. Why is she there?

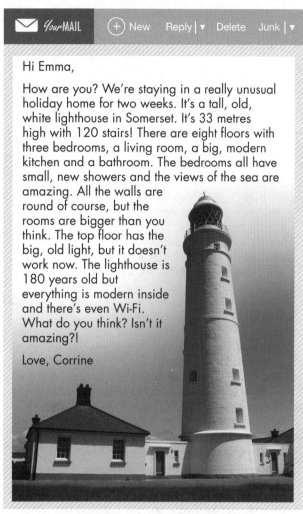

> Hi Emma,
>
> How are you? We're staying in a really unusual holiday home for two weeks. It's a tall, old, white lighthouse in Somerset. It's 33 metres high with 120 stairs! There are eight floors with three bedrooms, a living room, a big, modern kitchen and a bathroom. The bedrooms all have small, new showers and the views of the sea are amazing. All the walls are round of course, but the rooms are bigger than you think. The top floor has the big, old light, but it doesn't work now. The lighthouse is 180 years old but everything is modern inside and there's even Wi-Fi. What do you think? Isn't it amazing?!
>
> Love, Corrine

2 Read the email again. What do these numbers mean?

1 120 = *stairs in the lighthouse*
2 8 = _____
3 2 = _____
4 180 = _____
5 33 = _____

Useful language Order of adjectives

3 Read the email again. Write the adjectives.

1 a _____*tall*____ , _____ , _____ lighthouse
2 a _____ , _____ kitchen
3 _____ , _____ showers
4 the _____ , _____ light

4 Put the words in order to make sentences.

1 old / There's / tall / wardrobe / a / white
There's a tall, old, white wardrobe.

2 has got / living room / lamp / small / a / The / yellow / modern
_____

3 has got / a / bed / My / old / bedroom / large
_____

4 red and blue / The / got / four / big / pillows / bed's / new
_____

5 on his desk / a / photo / tiny / black and white / old / There's
_____

> **WRITING TIP**
>
> Make it better! ✓ ✓ ✓
> Use comparatives and superlatives to describe the things in your house.
> *My sister's bedroom is bigger than mine.*

5 Complete the sentences with the comparative or superlative form of the adjectives in brackets.

1 The bathrooms are *smaller than* the bedrooms. (small)
2 My parents have got _____ bedroom in the house. (large)
3 The wardrobe is _____ my bathroom! (big)
4 The furniture in her house is _____ the furniture in my house. (modern)
5 The apartment has got _____ views of the city. (beautiful)

6 Complete the sentences with two or three adjectives to describe the rooms in your house.

1 We've got a ___*small, new*___ kitchen.
2 There's a _____ bedroom.
3 There's a _____ living room.
4 I've got a _____ bathroom.

Writing

7 **Which of these sentences does <u>not</u> give an opinion?**

1 The house is really unusual.
2 The gardens are really beautiful.
3 There are three large bedrooms.
4 It's really relaxing to walk on the beach near the house.

8 **Read Corrine's email again and tick (✓) the information she includes.**

a what rooms there are ☐
b the number of bedrooms ☐
c what her favourite room is and why ☐
d what she does in each room ☐
e how old/big the house is ☐
f interesting or unusual features/furniture ☐

PLAN

9 **Choose one of these holiday homes to write an email about. Use the information in Exercise 8 and make notes.**

a castle in England

a stone cottage in Ireland

a luxury flat in a big city

a houseboat in the Netherlands

WRITE

10 **Write the email. Look at page 49 of the Student's Book to help you.**

_____
_____
_____
_____
_____
_____
_____
_____
_____
_____
_____
_____

CHECK

11 **Check your writing. Can you say YES to these questions?**

• Is the information from Exercise 8 in your description?
• Do you use adjectives to describe the room and things in the place?
• Do you use comparative and superlative sentences?
• Do you give your opinion of the place, the rooms or the things?

Do you need to write a second draft?

Vocabulary
Things in the home

1 Match the words in the box to the definitions.

sink towel mirror blanket curtains pillow
wardrobe ~~carpet~~ shelf cupboard desk

1 This is on the floor. You walk on it.   _carpet_
2 You open these in the morning so
  you can see outside.   _____
3 This is on the bed. It's for your head.   _____
4 This is in the bathroom. You use it
  after a shower.   _____
5 This is in the bathroom. You can
  see yourself in it.   _____
6 You put all your clothes in here.   _____
7 You put plates, cups, glasses or food
  in here.   _____
8 This is on the bed. You use it when
  it's cold.   _____
9 You put books on this.   _____
10 This is in your bedroom. You do
  your homework here.   _____
11 This is in the kitchen. You wash dirty
  plates in here.   _____

Total: 10

Household appliances

2 Complete the sentences with words in the box.

dishwasher ~~washing machine~~ fridge heater
lamp cooker hairdryer freezer iron

1 Put the dirty clothes into the _washing machine_ .
2 It's cold! Turn on the _____ .
3 Take some ice out of the _____ .
4 Put the milk back in the _____ .
5 I'd like to cook dinner. Turn on the _____ .
6 Your hair is wet. Go and get the _____ .
7 Put the dirty plates into the _____ .
8 Oh no! I burned my shirt with the _____ !
9 I can't see. It's very dark. Turn on the _____ .

Total: 8

Language focus
Comparatives

3 Write comparative sentences.

1 London / Edinburgh (big)
  London is bigger than Edinburgh.
2 Cheetahs / elephants (fast)
  _____
3 The Amazon / the Danube (long)
  _____
4 The Arctic / Iceland (cold)
  _____
5 Sharks / dolphins (dangerous)
  _____
6 Hawaii / Alaska (warm)
  _____
7 Hotels / youth hostels (expensive)
  _____

Total: 6

Superlatives

4 Write sentences in the superlative.

1 Russia / big / country / in the world
  Russia is the biggest country in the world.

2 The cheetah / fast / animal in the world
  _____
3 The *Mona Lisa* / famous / painting in the world
  _____
4 The University of Al-Karaouine in Morocco / old /
  university in the world
  _____
5 The Himalayas / high / mountains in the world
  _____
6 The Australian box jellyfish / poisonous / creature
  in the world
  _____

Total: 5

must/mustn't, should/shouldn't

5 **Complete the sentences with *must, mustn't, should* or *shouldn't* and the verb.**

1 It's a good idea to get up early.
You __*should get*__ up early.

2 It isn't ok to talk in the library.
You _____ quiet in the library.

3 It is against the rules to eat sandwiches in the classroom.
We _____ sandwiches in the classroom.

4 It isn't a good idea to talk and eat at the same time.
You _____ _____ at the same time.

5 You can't use your mobile during a test.
You _____ your mobile during a test.

Total: 4

Language builder

6 **Complete the conversation with the missing words. Circle the correct options.**

Dear Becky,
We [1]_____ a wonderful time on our holiday in Australia. We [2]_____ at a beautiful beach hotel. It's [3]_____ than at home! I love [4]_____ in the ocean.
We [5]_____ snorkelling near the beach yesterday when we saw [6]_____ dolphins! I think they're [7]_____ sea creatures in the world! I took [8]_____ of pictures!
I [9]_____ remember to send you some photos. It's really important to be careful in the sun over here. They told us we [10]_____ wear hats all the time and we [11]_____ out in the middle of the day.
See you soon!
Angie

1 a have   **b 're having**   c do have
2 a stay   b 're staying   c stayed
3 a sunny   b sunniest   c sunnier
4 a swim   b swimming   c swam
5 a was   b were   c are
6 a much   b any   c some
7 a the beautiful b the most   c the more
                       beautiful   beautiful
8 a a lot   b some   c many
9 a must   b mustn't   c should
10 a should   b aren't   c mustn't
11 a aren't going b must go   c shouldn't
                                            go

Total: 10

Vocabulary builder

7 **Choose the correct word.**

1 My uncle's daughter is my ___*cousin*___ .
   a aunt   b cousin   c mother

2 We studied the rivers of France in _____ today.
   a Geography   b History   c Maths

3 Your bedroom is really _____ . Pick up all those things!
   a unfriendly b unfair   c untidy

4 He ran very fast but he couldn't _____ them.
   a climb   b chase   c catch

5 Is there any ice cream in the _____ ?
   a cooker   b freezer   c fridge

6 He plays the piano and the guitar. He's an amazing _____ .
   a dancer   b scientist   c musician

7 I think there are some biscuits in the _____ .
   a cupboard   b wardrobe   c sink

8 Where's the _____ ? I'm going to lie down on the sofa.
   a carpet   b blanket   c towel

9 We're _____ in the park at the moment. Do you want to come?
   a walk   b walking   c doing

10 When the sun _____ we were all sleeping in our beds.
   a put up   b went up   c came up

Total: 9

Speaking

8 **Circle the correct options.**

Mum: Tom, [1]**can** / shall you help me in the kitchen?

Tom: OK. [2]**Do / Shall** I make the salad?

Mum: Yes, please, and [3]**can / shall** you do me a favour and take the dog out for a walk after dinner?

Tom: Sorry, I [4]**can't / don't**. I need to finish my homework. [5]**I'll / I ask** Sue.

Mum: That's OK. [6]**I'll / Shall** I do it.

Tom: [7]**Shall / Could** I tell Sue and Dad it's time for dinner?

Mum: Yes, please.

Total: 6

Total: 58

Comparatives and superlatives

Remember that:
• with short adjectives we add **-er** or **-est**.
• with long adjectives we use **more** or **the most**.

1 **Find and correct five more mistakes with comparatives and superlatives.**

Louisa:	What do you think of my new bedroom? It's ~~more bigger~~ ___bigger___ than my old room.
Izzie:	It's great! I love the big windows. It's more lighter than your old room too.
Louisa:	Yes. And I've got some new furniture. Do you like it?
Izzie:	Yes, it's moderner, isn't it? The old stuff was … well, more traditional.
Louisa:	I know, it was awful! I had the most old wardrobe in the world!
Izzie:	This one's much more nicer. You've got loads of space for all your clothes.
Louisa:	And come look at the view from the window. It's the beautifullest view in town.

must/mustn't, should/shouldn't

Remember, we use the infinitive without **to** after **should** and **must**.
✓ *You **should avoid** watching TV.*
✗ *You should to avoid watching TV.*
✓ *You **mustn't eat** a big meal before going to bed.*
✗ *You mustn't eating a big meal before going to bed.*

2 **Are the sentences correct? Correct the incorrect sentences.**

Six tips for exam success
1 You should ~~to~~ make a timetable of all the work you need to do.
2 You must getting at least 8 hours of sleep every night.
3 You shouldn't work late in the evening.
4 You must to remember to take a break.
5 You should going for a walk every day.
6 You mustn't forget to eat!
7 You should to drink a lot of water.

Prepositions of place

Remember that:
• we use **in** with rooms, towns and countries.
✓ *Maisie lives **in** the USA.*
• we use **on** with surfaces, e.g. *floor, wall, table*.
✓ *There is a computer **on** my desk.*
• we usually use **at** with buildings, e.g. *school, home*.
✓ *We stayed **at** a very unusual hotel.*

3 **Complete the sentences with at, in or on.**
1 ___In___ the kitchen, there's a fridge, a cooker and a dishwasher.
2 There is a library at school, but I prefer to do my homework _____ home.
3 I like the picture _____ the wall in the bedroom.
4 When it's cold, I put a blanket _____ the bed.
5 There's a lamp _____ the table in the living room.
6 I bought a beautiful mirror _____ San Francisco.

Spell it right! Comparative adjectives

Remember that:
• with short adjectives (one syllable) ending in vowel + consonant, we double the final consonant and add **-er** to form the comparative.
His bedroom is big. → *His bedroom is **bigger** than mine.*
• we do not use **more** or **very** before comparative adjectives ending in **-er**.
✓ *His bedroom is **bigger** than mine.*
✗ *His bedroom is more bigger than mine.*
✗ *His bedroom is very bigger than mine.*
• with long adjectives (two syllables +) we use **more** before the adjective.
Their house is beautiful. → *Their house is **more** beautiful than ours.*
• with adjectives that have two syllables and end in -y, we remove the -y and add **-ier**.
Your garden is pretty. → *Your garden is **prettier** than ours.*

4 **Write the comparative forms of the adjectives.**
1 cold ___colder___
2 expensive _____
3 tidy _____
4 comfortable _____
5 small _____
6 relaxing _____
7 high _____
8 easy _____

5 Visions of the future

Vocabulary
Computer words

1 ★ Use the pictures to find eight more computer words in the word search.

m	e	m	o	r	y	s	t	i	c	k	p
i	t	o	u	c	h	s	c	r	e	e	n
c	i	u	e	e	c	v	w	h	p	y	e
r	m	s	f	h	k	o	p	e	h	b	x
o	o	e	c	h	p	l	a	p	t	o	p
c	r	o	j	m	e	t	p	u	h	a	r
h	g	a	t	m	l	o	p	t	b	r	i
i	n	b	u	r	w	b	u	k	u	d	n
p	a	s	g	h	t	t	a	b	l	e	t
q	o	s	m	a	r	t	p	h	o	n	e
p	r	b	u	i	e	s	c	m	u	e	r

2 ★★ Complete the sentences with the words from Exercise 1.

1 I lost my *memory stick* with our school project on it, but later I found it in my jeans pocket.
2 It's easier to write emails with a _____ than on a touchscreen.
3 Now most phones have a _____ without buttons. You put your finger on the icons instead.
4 My mum hasn't got a _____ because she only uses a phone to make calls.
5 I like my _____ because the touchscreen is bigger than on a smartphone.
6 Our _____ can scan things and make photocopies too. It's amazing.
7 I take my _____ on holiday because my computer is too heavy and I haven't got a tablet.
8 You don't need a _____ with a tablet.
9 Without a _____ , computers, laptops and tablets don't work.

3 ★★★ Jack has got five of the things from Exercise 1. Read what he says and complete the table.

1 I've got one of these. It's bigger than a tablet but I can use it to do more things.
2 I haven't got one of these but my father has. He loves it because it's much smaller than a laptop!
3 Of course I've got one of these – a new one with a really good camera. I made my first call on it yesterday!
4 I had one of these but it broke. I don't miss it because I don't usually print anything anyway.
5 I've got one of these. It's really useful because you can use it on any computer but I think it's full because I've got a lot of photos on it!
6 Yes, I've also got one of these little things. It's from an old computer.

Jack has got ...	Jack hasn't got ...
a laptop	

4 ★★★ Which of these things do you and your friends use? When do you use them? Write about five of them.

> memory stick   mouse   laptop   touchscreen
> tablet   printer   smartphone

Most of my friends use a memory stick to put school projects and other homework on. We can take them home and back to school to show to other people.

Language focus 1

will/won't, may/might

1 ★ **Complete the rules in the grammar table.**

1	We use *will* and *won't* for **predictions / intentions**.
2	We use *may* and *might* to talk about **possibilities / things we are sure about**.
3	We use *will / won't / might / may* + **infinitive without *to* / infinitive with *to***.
4	We form the question with *will / do* + subject + *will / infinitive*.

2 ★ **Complete the predictions about the future. Use the verbs in the box.**

> be (x2) celebrate find go live need
> study use

1 Children __won't go__ (✗) to school every day. They _____ (✓) at home on their computers.

2 People _____ (✓) longer. Most people _____ (✓) their hundredth birthday.

3 Cars _____ (✗) a driver anymore. They _____ (✓) a computer to drive.

4 Scientists _____ (✓) life on other planets.

5 The weather _____ (✗) how it is now. There _____ (✓) a big climate change.

3 ★★ **Put the words in the correct order to make interview questions.**

Adnan, you're a millionaire at the age of 18.

1 with the money / you / What / will / do / ?
What will you do with the money?

2 type / will / car / What / you / of / buy / ?
_____

3 trophies / any / Will / your team / win / this season / ?
_____

4 How / score / goals / will / many / you / this season / ?
_____

5 you / will / Where / be / ten years from now / ?
_____

4 ★★ **Complete the sentences with *will / won't / may / might* and the verbs in brackets. Then match them with the questions in Exercise 3.**

a I hope I*'ll be* married and I_____ lots of kids. I love kids! (be, have)   *5*

b I don't know. I _____ more than last year, but maybe not. (score)   ___

c I'm not sure. I _____ a car and a house, but I probably _____ it all. I _____ some for the future. (buy, not spend, save)   ___

d Of course we _____ ! I think this team _____ the league and the cup! (win, win)   ___

e I _____ a sports car, but I'm not sure. I _____ before I pass my driving test! (get, decide)   ___

5 ★★★ **Complete the predictions of the food scientist with *will/won't/might/might not* and the verbs in brackets.**

> I think our food [1] __will taste__ (taste) the same but we definitely [2]_____ (not produce) it the same way. Producing meat is very expensive so we [3]_____ (not eat) animal meat in the future – I'm not sure. In fact, scientists [4]_____ (produce) our meat. Who knows? People [5]_____ (find) new things to eat so we [6]_____ (catch) different types of fish but I don't think people in Europe [7]_____ (eat) insects. I think we [8]_____ definitely _____ (eat) less meat than we do now.

Explore suffixes *-ful* and *-less*

6 ★★ **Complete the definitions with the words in the box.**

> beautiful useless wonderful painful
> ~~careless~~ hopeless

1 A person who does not look after their things is *careless* .

2 When a part of your body hurts, it is _____.

3 A situation is _____ when there is nothing you can do to make it better.

4 Something is _____ when it doesn't work or it doesn't do what you need it do to.

5 _____ things or people look good.

6 _____ means very good.

Listening and vocabulary

Technology verbs + prepositions

1 ★ **Match the verbs in the box with the definitions.**

> click on   sign in   scroll down   shut down
> ~~turn down~~   turn on   turn up   log on

1 make something quieter   *turn down*
2 move a web page while you're
   reading   _____
3 start a machine   _____
4 choose something on the screen   _____
5 turn off a computer   _____
6 make something louder   _____
7 enter a password to start your
   computer   _____
8 enter a password to read your
   emails or see an online account   _____

2 ★★ **Complete the text with the correct form of the verbs from Exercise 1.**

> **Mum:** Where's that video you were telling me about?
> **Liam:** Let's see. Yes, that's the page. Now ¹*scroll down* to the bottom and then ² _____ the link that says 'Summer camp video'.
> **Mum:** Great. Thanks.
> **Liam:** I'm going to bed. Don't forget to ³ _____ the computer when you finish.
> **Mum:** Liam, can you ⁴ _____ the music, please? It's very loud.
> **Liam:** Oh, Mum!
> **Mum:** Actually, you should stop the music – it's late and you have to go to bed.
> **Liam:** But Mum! I just ⁵ _____ it _____ five minutes ago!

Listening

3 ★ 🔊 **05** **Listen to Mark talking to Liz about a programme he watched on TV. What was the programme about? Who talks about the things in the pictures?**

1 remote control

2 fingerprint

3 standby

4 power cut

4 ★★ 🔊 **05** **Listen again and circle the correct options.**

1 Mark watched a (TV programme) / film about smarthomes.
2 You **can / can't** control everything in your house when you're not at home.
3 Bill Gates spent $100,000,000 on his **TV / smarthome**.
4 The lights turn **off / on** automatically when you walk into a room.
5 You can turn on the bathroom shower from the **living room / bedroom**.
6 You **need / don't need** a key to get into your smarthome.
7 Liz's ideal home is as **simple / beautiful** as possible.

Language focus 2

First conditional

1 ★ (Circle) the correct words in the grammar table.

1	We use the first conditional to talk about the **present** / **future** result of an action or situation.
2	We use the **present simple** / **will** + infinitive for the action or situation clause, and **present simple** / **will** + infinitive for the result clause.

2 ★★ **Match the sentence beginnings (1–6) with the sentence endings (a–f).**

1 We won't hear this video ___*b*___
2 You'll see the link to her blog ___
3 If they give the students tablets, ___
4 If I find your memory stick, ___
5 Will you buy me a smartphone ___
6 What do you think will happen to the computer ___

a if we shut it down now?
b if the teacher doesn't turn up the volume.
c studying will be more fun.
d if you scroll down the page.
e if I pass all my exams?
f I'll ring you.

3 ★★ **Complete the first conditional sentences with the correct form of the verbs in brackets.**

1 If students ____*use*____ (use) computers for all their schoolwork, they __*will forget*__ (forget) how to write by hand!
2 If we _____ (not practise) writing by hand, what _____ (we / do) in the exams?
3 I think a new laptop _____ (be) cheaper if you _____ (buy) it online.
4 I _____ (not finish) my Science project tonight if I _____ (not find) my memory stick.
5 _____ (you / remember) to turn everything off if I _____ (go) to bed now?
6 If he _____ (not turn down) the music, I think the neighbours _____ (be) angry. But it _____ (not be) a problem if he _____ (put) his headphones on.
7 How _____ (they / get) home from the concert, if there _____ (not be) any buses after eleven?

4 ★★★ **Match the sentence halves.**

1 I / go to the cinema / this weekend
2 The touchscreen / not work
3 If / turn off / the TV
4 If / you / not / turn down / the music
5 If / we / not buy / the tickets soon

a you / study better
b we / not get / seats at the concert
c if / Helen / come / with me
d the neighbours / be / angry
e if / you / wear / gloves

5 **Write conditional sentences with the information in Exercise 4.**

1 *I'll go to the cinema this weekend if Helen comes with me.*
2 _____
3 _____
4 _____
5 _____

Explore phrasal verbs 1

6 ★★ **Complete the text with the correct form of the phrasal verbs in the box.**

take off   put on   sit down   ~~get up~~   look for

Carl ¹___*got up*___ early again. He ²_____ at his desk. What a mess! He ³_____ his glasses but he couldn't find them. He pushed some papers and they fell on the floor. His glasses were under the papers. He ⁴_____ them _____ and turned up the music. He tried to work but he was tired. He ⁵_____ his glasses, threw them on the desk and went to sleep.

Reading

1 ★ **Read the text about cars in the future. How are they different from the cars we have now?**

WHERE'S THE DRIVER? ▶▶▶

Imagine going into town to go shopping. You arrive at the station. The shopping centre is a 20-minute walk away, but you have a better idea. You get in a pod – a small car. You can't drive, but that's no problem, because the pod doesn't need a driver. It has a computer! There's a screen, so you surf the web or play computer games. Is this science fiction? No, it will soon be reality.

A hundred driverless pods will soon be on the road in the British town of Milton Keynes. They will travel on the pavement, but their special computer program will use GPS, HD cameras and sensors to navigate safely. Each pod can carry two people and travel at a maximum speed of about 19 kph. They save time and are better for the environment, because they don't cause pollution.

Google is also developing a 'self-driving car' by adapting normal cars. The US states of Nevada, Florida and California permit driverless cars on normal roads with other traffic.

So, in the future you may have the opportunity to download an app onto your smartphone and call a driverless pod to take you where you want to go. Another option, of course, is to walk!

Google self-driving car

2 ★★ **Match the words from the text with their definitions.**

> environment   science fiction   pollution   ~~imagine~~   navigate

1 to picture something in your mind   *imagine*
2 a type of book or film usually about the future, space or other planets   _____
3 move around something or find the right direction   _____
4 the air, water and land on and in which people and animals live   _____
5 something that happens when the air or water is not clean   _____

3 ★★ **Read the text again. Mark the sentences *true (T)* or *false (F)*. Correct the false sentences.**

1 Driverless cars use a computer to drive the car.   *T*
2 If you can't drive, you can't go in a pod.   _____
3 The pods in Milton Keynes will be on the road with other cars.   _____
4 The pods won't go very fast.   _____
5 Driverless cars won't help the environment.   _____
6 Driverless cars can travel on the road in some parts of the US.   _____
7 One day people will phone driverless taxis.   _____

4 ★★★ **What do you think of driverless cars? Why are they a good idea? Can you think of any problems with them? Write four or five sentences.**

_____
_____
_____
_____
_____

Writing

An opinion essay

1 Read the question and the opinion essay. Does the writer agree or disagree with the question?

> How do you imagine your future? Will your life be very different from your parents'? Write an essay with the title: *'My life will be the same as my parents' lives. Do you agree?'*
>
> Give us your opinion.

Most people agree that nowadays life is very different from twenty years ago, so I don't think that my life will be exactly the same as my parents' lives. However, I don't think that it will be completely different.

For example, I'm sure that I will go to university, like my parents. If I can, I will look for a good job near where they live. It isn't as easy as it was, but I'm optimistic.

Some people say that the world is a smaller place because of the Internet, while others believe that young people stay at home for longer. In my opinion, I'm more adventurous than my parents. When I finish university, I will probably work abroad for a while. My parents never did that!

In conclusion, I think I will have more opportunities than my parents, but it might be more difficult to find a secure job.

2 Read the essay again. Tick (✓) the opinions from the essay.
1 Life is different now from in the past. ☐
2 The writer's life will be the same as his/her parents' lives. ☐
3 It's not difficult to find a job. ☐
4 The Internet changes how we see the world. ☐
5 There will be more possibilities in the future. ☐

3 Look back at the essay. Complete these phrases.
1 _However_ , I don't think
2 _____ my opinion,
3 _____ people say that
4 _____ people agree that
5 _____ believe that
6 _____ conclusion,
7 _____ example,
8 I'm _____ that

4 Read the essay. (Circle) the correct options.

1(Some people say that)/ Other people say that the future will be better than the present. 2Some people say that / Other people say that it will be worse, but 3most people agree that / in conclusion it will be very different.
4I'm sure that / Other people say that my life will be very different in the future. 5However, / For example, many things will be the same. 6In my opinion, / Most people agree that my family and friends will always be important.
7In conclusion, / However, nobody knows what life will be like in the future. 8For example, / However, isn't that exciting?

5 Complete the sentences with the correct comparative or superlative form of the words in brackets.
1 _The most important_ (important) thing nowadays is to get a good education.
2 I think I'm _____ (adventurous) person in my family.
3 It's _____ (difficult) to find a job today than in the past.
4 We can find information much _____ (quick) than in the past.
5 I'm sure that people now aren't _____ (tall) than they were in the past.

Writing

> **WRITING TIP**
>
> Make it better! ✓ ✓ ✓
> We use *when* to say we are sure that something happened or will happen. We use *if* to say we are not sure something will happen.
> *I'll cook dinner when I get home.*
> *I'll buy a tablet if my parents give me birthday money.*

6 **Complete the sentences with *when* or *if*. Sometimes both words are possible.**

1 ____*When*____ my parents were younger, they travelled less than I do.
2 I'll probably get a good job _____ I leave university.
3 _____ I study at university, I'll probably go to Cambridge.
4 I know I'll need to speak English _____ I'm older.
5 _____ I get a job in a big company, I will work abroad for a few years.

> **WRITING TIP**
>
> Make it better! ✓ ✓ ✓
> Explain your opinion: give reasons or examples.
> *I think life was difficult for my grandparents because they had to work very hard.*

7 **Look at the essay again. Find examples of when the writer gives reasons or examples for his/her opinion.**

For example,

8 **Tick (✓) the sentence that does not give reasons for the opinions.**

1 Young people are more adventurous because we travel more than our parents did. ☐
2 Technology will help us. For example, the Internet will give us more information. ☐
3 I'm optimistic about the future because I believe that the world will be a better place. ☐
4 We don't know what the world will be like in the future. ☐
5 Most people agree that life for young people is easier in some ways. For example, it is easier to study or go to university. ☐

9 **Read the opinion essay again and order the paragraphs.**

A arguments for the statement ___
B introduction and your opinion _1_
C conclusion and final opinion ___
D arguments against the statement ___

PLAN

10 **You are going to write an opinion essay for the task in Exercise 1. Use the paragraphs in Exercise 9 and make notes.**

WRITE

11 **Write the opinion essay. Look at page 61 of the Student's Book to help you.**

_____
_____
_____
_____
_____
_____
_____
_____
_____
_____
_____
_____

CHECK

12 **Check your writing. Can you say YES to these questions?**

• Did you use the essay structure in Exercise 9?
• Do you use comparative forms to compare your life to your parents' lives?
• Do you use *when* and *if* sentences correctly?
• Do you give reasons for and examples of your opinion?

Do you need to write a second draft?

Vocabulary
Computer words

1 Circle the correct words.

A ¹tablet / printer is easy to carry. It has a ²touchscreen / smartphone so you don't need a mouse or a ³keyboard / microphone.

A ⁴laptop / tablet is bigger and has a thin ⁵keyboard / memory stick, a wireless ⁶mouse / microchip, and a large ⁷smartphone / touchscreen. You can use the ⁸keyboard / printer to make copies.

Total: 7

Technology verbs + prepositions

2 Circle the correct options.
1 Sign on to / in to your account.
2 Log up / on to your computer.
3 Turn on / over the laptop.
4 Scroll down / in the web page.
5 Click down / on the icon.
6 Turn in / up the volume.
7 Shut down / up the computer when you finish.

Total: 6

Language focus
will/won't, may/might

3 Complete the text with *will, won't, may (not)* or *might (not)*.

What ¹____will____ our homes be like in the future? In the homes of the future, there ²_____ be any housework to do, and it's possible that there ³_____ be any cooking because everyone ⁴_____ have robot helpers to clean the house and cook the meals. The fridges ⁵_____ connect to the Internet and tell you what food to buy. The alarm clock ⁶_____ read your daily schedule and know what time you need to get up for work. You ⁷_____ drive to work, the car ⁸_____ drive itself or we ⁹_____ even have flying cars! It's possible.

Total: 8

First conditional

4 Circle the correct options.
1 They won't / don't pass the exam if they don't know how to speak English.
2 If you help me with my homework, I will / don't help you with your computer.
3 If you will use / use your smartphone in class, the teacher might send you home.
4 My mum won't buy me a smartphone if I don't / won't pass all my exams.
5 Will they send you an email if you get / will get the job?
6 If you bring / will bring your smartphone, I won't need my camera.
7 Will / Do you fix my computer if I take it to your house today?

Total: 6

5 Complete the sentences using *will/won't* and the words in brackets.
1 ___I will buy___ (I / buy) some headphones tomorrow if they have some cheap ones in the shop.
2 If Alison doesn't go to the party, _____ (Frank / go) either. They go everywhere together!
3 Ben said _____ (he / put) the photo on his blog, if he has time this weekend.
4 If you don't phone your mum, _____ (she / be / angry).
5 Do you think _____ (the teacher / give) us an exam tomorrow, if we ask her not to?

Total: 4

Language builder

6 (Circle) the correct options.

Martina:	Is that a new smartphone?	
Steve:	Yes, it ¹_____. I ²_____ it for my birthday and I ³_____ how to use it.	
Martina:	Nice! Does it have a lot of apps?	
Steve:	Yes, it does. But in my opinion, it hasn't got ⁴_____ games. I ⁵_____ download some more.	
Martina:	Is it ⁶_____ than your old phone?	
Steve:	Yes, but it ⁷_____ as fast as those super-expensive ones.	
Martina:	My mum said she'll give me a smartphone if I ⁸_____ my exam.	
Steve:	That's great! You ⁹_____ like some of these new games.	
Martina:	Yes, but you know we ¹⁰_____ use them at school.	
Steve:	Yes. The teacher said we ¹¹_____ use smartphones in the lesson.	

1	a does	**ⓑ is**	c was
2	a get	b am getting	c got
3	a learn	b 'm learning	c will learn
4	a enough	b the	c some
5	a prefer	b like	c might
6	a fast	b faster	c fastest
7	a is	b isn't	c doesn't
8	a pass	b will pass	c am passing
9	a do	b might	c should
10	a don't	b shouldn't	c won't
11	a must	b should	c mustn't

Total: 10

Vocabulary builder

7 (Circle) the correct options.

1 The police _____ the thieves down the street.
  a jumped   **ⓑ chased**   c ran
2 We keep ice cream in the _____ .
  a dishwasher   b freezer   c microwave
3 Use the _____ to type your password.
  a printer   b mouse   c keyboard
4 You can open the apps from the _____ .
  a keyboard   b microchip   c touchscreen
5 You can sit on a _____ .
  a sofa   b wardrobe   c cupboard
6 The thief _____ into the bank through a window.
  a climbed   b caught   c hid
7 You can cook spaghetti on the _____ .
  a fridge   b cooker   c heater
8 We were late so we ate our lunch _____ .
  a quickly   b sleepily   c slowly
9 I closed the _____ and went to bed.
  a blanket   b pillow   c curtains
10 Scroll _____ the web page to see your emails.
  a down   b in   c over
11 The road was icy so I walked very _____ .
  a easily   b quickly   c carefully

Total: 10

Speaking

8 **Complete the conversation with the words in the box.**

You have to ...   How do I ...   First   Now   ~~work~~

Jenny:	Is that a new tablet?
Sue:	Yes! Do you want to try it?
Jenny:	How does it ¹ _**work**_ ?
Sue:	²_____ , you need to press the power button.
Jenny:	OK. What do I do next?
Sue:	³_____ , type in the password.
Jenny:	⁴_____ check my email?
Sue:	⁵_____ press the icon.
Jenny:	I see! Thanks!

Total: 4

Total: 55

will/won't, may/might

Remember, we use the infinitive without *to* after **will**, **won't**, **may** and **might**.

✓ *Online friends **won't replace** real friends.*
✗ ~~*Online friends won't replaced real friends.*~~
✓ *The council **might ban** cars in the city centre.*
✗ ~~*The council might banned cars in the city centre.*~~

1 **Correct four more mistakes in the conversation.**

Juan:	What are you going to do in the summer?
Marta:	I'm not sure, but I might ~~visited~~ ^visit^ my pen friend in Ireland. What about you?
Juan:	I'll definitely travelled to Europe.
Marta:	Oh, where will you go?
Juan:	I'll probably flew to England, and I might studied English there.
Marta:	That's a great idea! Well, I might saw you in London if I go there. That would be fantastic!

First conditional

Remember that:

• we use the first conditional to talk about the future result of an action or situation.
• we use **if** + subject + the present simple in the action/situation clause. We do not use **will/won't** in the same clause as **if**.
  ✓ ***If I'm*** *late, **I will send** you a text.*
  ✗ ~~*If I will be late, I will send you a text.*~~
• we put a comma after the *if* clause when it comes at the beginning of the sentence.
  ✓ ***If I'm*** *late, **I will send** you a text.*
  ✗ ~~*I will send you a text if I'm late.*~~

2 **Are the sentences correct? Correct the incorrect sentences.**

1 If you will come with me, I'll be very happy.
   If you come with me, I'll be very happy.

2 If I find your mobile I'll bring it to school tomorrow.
   _____

3 Lucy will be angry with me if she will find out.
   _____

4 I think it will be more fun if you come too.
   _____

5 If I won't finish my homework, I'll be in trouble.
   _____

Computer words

Remember that:

• we usually use **the** before *Internet*.
  ✓ *I enjoy surfing **the** Internet.*
• we use **on**, not *in* or *with*, to talk about using the **Internet** or a **computer**.
  ✓ *I like playing **on my computer**.*
  ✗ ~~*I like playing with my computer.*~~
• we usually use **a** or **the** with **computer**.
  ✓ *I want to learn how to use **a computer**.*
  ✗ ~~*I want to learn how to use computer.*~~
  ✓ *I really enjoy playing **on the computer**.*
  ✗ ~~*I really enjoy playing on computer.*~~

3 **Find six more mistakes in the text.**

I got ^a^ new computer for my birthday. I needed computer because I like using Internet and playing games. Computer is useful for homework and there are lots of useful programs in the computer too. I've put the computer in my bedroom. When my friend visits me, we can play games with the computer. That's great, because he hasn't got computer at home.

Phrasal verbs

Remember that:

• we use **on** and **off** with **take**, and **down** and **up** with **turn** for some meanings.
• we use **on** to talk about wearing something or making a piece of equipment start working.
  ✓ *He put **on** his coat and left the house.*
• we use **off** to talk about not wearing something or making a piece of equipment stop working.
  ✓ *You should take **off** your shoes when you go in.*
• we use **down** to talk about making something less, and **up** to talk about making something more.
  ✓ *You can turn **down** the music if it's too loud.*
  ✓ *You can turn **up** the music if it's too quiet.*

4 **Add *on*, *off*, *down* or *up* to each sentence.**

1 She turned ^on^ the TV to watch the news.
2 It was cold outside, so he put his hat.
3 Remember to turn the lights when you leave.
4 She took her coat because it was wet.
5 They turned the music because it was too loud.
6 Please turn the TV, it's not loud enough.

6 Life choices

Vocabulary

Life events

1 ★ **Match the life events in the box to the definitions.**

> get married   start school   leave home
> go to university   have children   ~~leave school~~
> take a year out   be born   get a job
> learn to drive

1 You can do this at 16 in most of Europe, but in Germany it's 18. *leave school*
2 You need a teacher for this … and a car, of course! _____
3 The first event in life! _____
4 Lots of people do this because it helps you to get a better job. _____
5 We do this to earn money. _____
6 Some people do this so they can travel or work between school and university. _____
7 Couples do this when they want to be together forever. _____
8 Most children do this between the ages of three and six. _____
9 When this happens, you become a parent! _____
10 Everyone has to do this. You can't live with your parents forever! _____

2 ★★ **Complete the sentences with the correct form of the words from Exercise 1.**

1 Johnny Depp and Josh Hutcherson were both ____*born*____ in the state of Kentucky, USA.
2 Prince William learned to _____ when he was sixteen.
3 Salma Hayek went to _____ in Mexico City to study a degree in International Relations.
4 The actor Benedict Cumberbatch _____ a year out to teach English in Tibet.
5 Keira Knightley got _____ to her husband in the south of France.

6 Daniel Craig _____ home when he was sixteen to join the National Youth Theatre.
7 Before she was famous, Madonna got a _____ at a fast food restaurant.
8 Brad Pitt and Angelina Jolie had twins in 2008, and now they have six _____ .
9 Ben Affleck and Matt Damon started the same _____ at the same time but Affleck was in a different class.
10 The singer Katy Perry _____ school when she was 15.

3 ★★★ **Complete the second sentence so that it has the same meaning as the first. Use the life events in Exercise 1.**

1 My dad taught me to drive in his old car.
I *learned to drive in my dad's old car.*
2 I was quite happy to say goodbye to all my teachers.
I wasn't sad when I … _____
3 I'm not sure if I'm ready to look after children.
I don't know if I should … _____
4 I haven't lived in my parents' house since I was 21 years old.
I … _____
5 My first day at school was the day after my fifth birthday.
I … _____
6 My wedding was 10 years ago.
My wife and I … _____
7 I started studying Engineering when I was 18 years old.
I … _____
8 My sister's birthday is on 8 June.
My sister … _____
9 Between school and university I travelled around South America.
_____ … and travelled around South America.
10 After school I started working at a computer company.
After school I … _____

4 ★★★ **What do you know about celebrities? Choose one or more and write about their life events. Write at least five sentences.**

Taylor Swift was born in December 1989. She left school at 14 to become a singer.

Language focus 1

be going to

1 ★ **Choose the correct words in the grammar table.**

1	We use *be going to* for **future intentions / offers**.
2	They are going **have / to have** a party.
3	**We aren't / We not** going to come to your house tonight.
4	**Are you going / Are going you** to leave early?
5	Yes, **I'm going / I am**. No, he **isn't going / isn't**.

2 ★★ **Complete the sentences with *be going to* and the verbs in brackets.**

1 They*'re going to cycle* across Russia for charity. (cycle)
2 She _____ until she's 30. (not get married)
3 He _____ a birthday party this year. (not have)
4 We _____ my cousins this summer. (not visit)
5 She _____ Geography at university. (study)
6 They _____ camping with their friends this summer. (go)
7 Theo _____ in a bank when he leaves school. (not work)

will vs. be going to

3 ★★ (Circle) **the correct words. Use *be going to* for plans and intentions and *will* for predictions.**

Tiger x2

2022 is the Chinese year of the tiger, but the World Wildlife Fund (WWF) believes that wild tigers **¹are going to / (will)** disappear completely in the next 50 years. That's why this year WWF **²is going to / will** start a new project called *Tiger x2*. With this project, the WWF **³are going to / will** try to protect 12 important areas where tigers live, and they **⁴are going to / will** use new technology to find tigers so they can stop people from killing them. Experts think this new technology **⁵is going to / will** be very important, but WWF also predicts that it **⁶isn't going to / won't** be easy. Projects like this always need a lot of money, so the news that the Leonardo DiCaprio Foundation **⁷is going to / will** help save the tigers is fantastic! They think this **⁸is going to / will** make a big difference to the tigers.

4 ★★★ **Write sentences about the plans and intentions of the people in the table.**

Danny	Sarah	Sinead
✓ climb trees in the park	✗ play tennis with Danny	✓ study for her exam
Phil	**Glen**	**Mike**
✓ invite Sinead to the cinema	✗ tidy his room	✗ call Sarah

1 *Danny's going to climb trees in the park.*
2 _____
3 _____
4 _____
5 _____
6 _____

Explore phrasal verbs 2

5 ★★ **Complete the diary entry with the correct form of the phrasal verbs in the box.**

grow up ~~find out~~ write down go out try on get on get off

I ¹**found out** what I'm going to do tomorrow. Yesterday my mum came into my room and said: 'Tomorrow we're going to ² _____ shopping. We're going to ³ _____ the bus and go into town. We're going to ⁴ _____ at Lion Road.' But why? I asked. 'We're going to buy some new school shoes for you,' she said. New shoes! I don't like shopping for shoes with my mum. We go to ten different shops and I ⁵ _____ one hundred different pairs. Why can't I go on my own? I asked. 'When you ⁶ _____ , you can buy your own shoes, I promise,' she said. That's why I'm ⁷ _____ this _____ – so I won't forget her promise!

Listening and vocabulary

Containers and materials

1 ★ **Match the words in the box with the pictures.**

> carton   cardboard box   glass jar   can   ~~plastic bag~~
> paper bag   crisp packet   plastic bottle

1 *plastic bag*

2 _____

3 _____

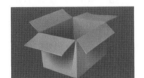

4 _____

5 _____

6 _____

7 _____

8 _____

2 ★★ **Complete the sentences with words from Exercise 1.**

1 Can I have a ____*can*____ of coke, please?
2 When I was young I made a house to play in. My 'house' was a big _____ !
3 How many _____ of milk have we got?
4 Many supermarkets charge money for a _____ now, so people bring their own bags.
5 Do you need that _____ ? I make jam at home and I need something to put it in.
6 Some shops put your shopping in a _____ because plastic bags are bad for the environment.
7 We buy more than 50 billion _____ of water every year, but we recycle only 20% of them.

Listening

3 ★★ 🔊 **06** **Listen to Amelia talk about taking a year out. Does she think it's a good idea?**

4 ★★ 🔊 **06** **Listen again and tick the correct sentences.**

1 A gap year is usually the year before university. ✓
2 Amelia is going to take a gap year.
3 Young people can work on eco projects in their gap year.
4 Living in a different culture is easy.
5 It's a good idea to do something connected to your future studies.
6 One of Amelia's friends is going to improve her Portuguese next year.
7 A gap year can help you to improve important life skills.
8 Universities don't like students to take a gap year.

Language focus 2

Present continuous for future

1 ★ (Circle) the correct word in the grammar table.

> We use the present continuous to talk about **present / future** arrangements.

2 ★★ Put the words in order to make sentences. Use contractions if possible.

1 They / the / are / housework / doing / on Sunday
They're doing the housework on Sunday.

2 am / Sonia / I / after school / seeing / not
_____

3 We / meeting / tomorrow morning / at / are / eight
_____

4 Two of / are / in June / leaving / my teachers
_____

5 not / this school / He / staying / at / is / next year
_____

6 She / driving test / taking / is / her / this afternoon
_____

3 ★★ Complete the text with the present continuous form of the verbs in the box.

> bring   drive   ~~arrive~~   not take   not stay   take

The players ¹*are arriving* at the airport at four o'clock. First, a coach ² _____ them here to the Town Hall. Then the mayor ³ _____ them outside with the cup at five o'clock. They ⁴ _____ there for a long time, because at 5.30 they ⁵ _____ through the city to the stadium in an open-top bus. This time the players ⁶ _____ the cup with them on the bus. They don't want any accidents.

4 ★★ Complete the conversation with the words in brackets.

A: ¹*Are you going* to the basketball match tomorrow? (you / go)

B: Yes, what time ² _____ ? (we / meet)

A: I don't know. I ³ _____ with you and Jody. My sister and I ⁴ _____ to the dentist at 6.30. (not come; go)

A: How ⁵ _____ to the match then? (you / get)

B: Mum ⁶ _____ me there after the dentist. (drive)

5 ★★★ Use the information in the table to write sentences with the present continuous in the order they will happen.

Brenda	meet Freddy at 3 o'clock
Freddy	go to cinema at 7 o'clock
Johnny	drive Freddy to the cinema
Dad	come home for lunch at 2 o'clock
Me (Chloe)	leave for football practice before Dad comes home

1 *I'm leaving for football practice.*
2 _____
3 _____
4 _____
5 _____

6 ★★★ Have you made any arrangements for the weekend? For next week? What are you doing? What aren't you doing? Write at least five sentences.

I'm not having my English class next Wednesday afternoon. I'm going to the dentist.

(E)xplore verbs with prepositions

7 ★★ Match the sentence beginnings (1–6) with the sentence endings (a–f).

1 Tomorrow at school, we're going to learn   *e*
2 How much are you going to pay   ___
3 When I woke up I was dreaming   ___
4 I don't want to watch TV so I'm going to listen   ___
5 I can't go out now because I'm waiting   ___
6 I don't want to spend more than £600   ___

a on a new computer.
b to some music for a while.
c for the car you're buying?
d about scoring a goal in the World Cup final!
e about the history of Poland.
f for my friend to arrive.

Reading

1 ★ **Read the text about two people and how their lives changed. What do they have in common?** Circle **the correct option.**

a They went from poor to rich. b They did something surprising. c They had an unhappy life.

Life choices

Mike

I was the first person in my family to go to university, and when I left I found a job in a bank in the city of London. At first I enjoyed it, and after ten years I had a good position and a great **salary**, but I hated it! I needed a more **rewarding** job, so I decided to become a teacher.

I started as a volunteer in a secondary school. It was **demanding** but fantastic. Now I'm doing a teacher training course and next week I'm starting teaching practice. Then I'm going to look for a permanent job. Classrooms need enthusiasm and creativity. I hope I can make a difference to the young people I'll teach. People think I'm mad, but I know it's the right **career** choice for me!

Kirsty

She left school at 16 and learned about food at her parents' health food shop. She had her son when she was 19. He was allergic to **dairy** and nuts, and Kirsty couldn't find any dairy-free ice cream he could eat. So she bought a cheap ice cream machine and made her own ice cream in her kitchen. Her son loved it, her family and friends loved it, and she decided to start a business. It soon became a big success.

Now you can buy her ice cream in most UK supermarkets, and soon she's taking it to the USA. Next year she's going to **launch** cheap, healthy meals you can buy in the supermarket. Her business is growing, and she will be a millionaire when her son starts secondary school.

2 ★★ **Complete the definitions with the words in bold in the text.**

1 The money that you earn in a year for your job is your ___*salary*___ .

2 Your _____ is all the different jobs that you do in your life.

3 When a company _____ a product, they sell it for the first time.

4 _____ products are foods like milk, cheese or yoghurt.

5 A _____ job is one that you like and that makes you feel good.

6 If something is _____ it is hard and needs a lot of your time and effort.

3 ★★ **Read the text in Exercise 1 again. Complete the sentences with Mike or Kirsty.**

1 ___*Mike*___ had a lot of money before.

2 _____ will be rich in the future.

3 _____ had no business experience.

4 _____ didn't like his/her career.

5 _____ went back to studying as an adult.

6 _____ has made a decision people don't understand.

7 _____ created something new.

4 ★★★ **Whose story was more surprising, Mike's or Kirsty's? Why? Do you know anyone who had a big change in their life? What did they do?**

Writing

A thank you email

1 **Read Hayley's email to her aunt. How did she help Hayley?**

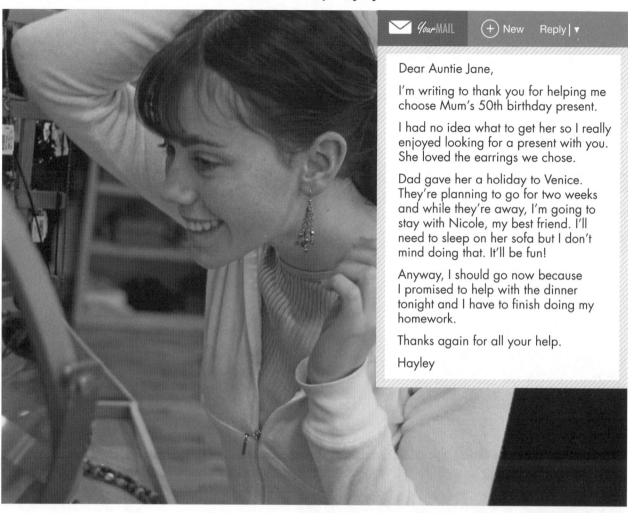

Dear Auntie Jane,

I'm writing to thank you for helping me choose Mum's 50th birthday present.

I had no idea what to get her so I really enjoyed looking for a present with you. She loved the earrings we chose.

Dad gave her a holiday to Venice. They're planning to go for two weeks and while they're away, I'm going to stay with Nicole, my best friend. I'll need to sleep on her sofa but I don't mind doing that. It'll be fun!

Anyway, I should go now because I promised to help with the dinner tonight and I have to finish doing my homework.

Thanks again for all your help.

Hayley

2 **Read the email again. Answer the questions.**
1 How old is Hayley's mum? _____
2 What did Hayley buy for her mum? _____
3 Where is her mum going with her dad? _____
4 Who is Nicole? _____
5 Where is Hayley going when her parents are on holiday? _____

Useful language Verb patterns ———

3 **Look back at Hayley's email. Complete the phrases with the words in the text.**
1 I really enjoyed *looking for a present with you* .
2 They're planning _____ .
3 I'll need _____ .
4 I don't mind _____ .
5 I promised _____ .
6 I have to finish _____ .

4 **Complete the sentences with the correct form of the verbs in the box below.**

help study watch play buy ~~take~~

1 My teacher is planning __*to take*__ our class on a school trip.
2 My brother enjoys _____ computer games with his friends.
3 I have an exam tomorrow so I need _____ tonight.
4 We finished _____ the film at 8 pm last night.
5 They promised _____ me a tablet for my birthday.
6 I don't mind _____ you with your homework.

Writing

5 Complete the sentences with the correct question words.

> where   how many   how   ~~what~~   when

1 It's my friend's party and I don't know ____*what*____ to wear.
2 My mum and dad are trying to decide _____ to go on holiday.
3 Let's talk about _____ to have the party – How about next Friday?
4 I'm writing to ask you _____ to make a very important decision in my life.
5 I'm not sure _____ people to invite to the party. I think 20 friends will be enough.

6 Circle the correct option.
1 I'd like to thank you **of /** **for** all your help.
2 I was hoping to talk **to / with** you about something.
3 My dad's thinking **to / of** taking my mum on a romantic weekend.
4 Did you hear **of / about** the present I got from Uncle Hugh?
5 I'm writing **to / for** you to say thanks.

> **WRITING TIP**
>
> Make it better! ✓ ✓ ✓
> Include different phrases to say thank you.
> *Thank you so much.*
> *It's very kind of you.*

7 Which of these is not a phrase to say thank you?
1 Thanks a lot!
2 I really appreciate it.
3 I'm writing to thank you for the beautiful present.
4 Did you say thanks to your mum?
5 Thank you so much for everything.

8 Look back at Hayley's email. Tick (✓) the information she includes.
1 the reason for writing ☐
2 what happened ☐
3 other news ☐
4 her aunt's health ☐
5 future plans ☐
6 phrases to say thank you ☐

PLAN

9 You are going to write a thank you email to a friend or family member who helped you. Choose one of the situations below. Then use the ideas in Exercise 8 and make notes.

_____ helped me with …

a a present
b a holiday
c a decision
d organising a party

WRITE

10 Write the thank you email. Look at page 71 of the Student's Book to help you.

_____
_____
_____
_____
_____
_____
_____
_____
_____
_____
_____
_____

CHECK

11 Check your writing. Can you say YES to these questions?
- Did you use the ideas in Exercise 8?
- Do you use the correct verb patterns?
- Do you use prepositions correctly?
- Do you use different phrases to say thank you?

Do you need to write a second draft?

Vocabulary
Life events

1 Match the sentence halves.

1 I want to travel around the world when I ...   _c_
2 I want to study Art when I go to ...   ___
3 I was 25 when my first child was ....   ___
4 I was 18 when I ...   ___
5 I want to buy a car but first, I need to learn ...   ___
6 After I leave university, I want to ...   ___
7 If I meet the right person, I'll probably get ...   ___

a to drive.
b left school.
c take a year out.
d university.
e get a job.
f married.
g born.

☐ Total: 6

Containers and materials

2 Write the words in the box under the correct picture. You can use some words more than once.

| bag bottle box can cardboard carton |
| crisp packet ~~glass jar~~ paper plastic |

1 _glass_ _jar_   2 _____ _____

3 _____ _____   4 _____ _____

5 _____   6 _____

7 _____ _____   8 _____ _____

☐ Total: 7

Language focus
be going to

3 Complete the conversation with the correct form of *be going to* and the verbs in brackets.

> **Jack:** What ¹ _are you going to do_ (you / do) this summer?
> **Rosie:** I ² _____ (work) on a farm. How about you? ³ _____ (you / do) anything special?
> **Jack:** Well, I ⁴_____ (not work)!
> **Rosie:** ⁵_____ (you / travel)?
> **Jack:** Yes, I am. My brother ⁶ _____ (sail) to Alaska and he ⁷_____ (take) me with him!
> **Rosie:** That sounds amazing!

☐ Total: 6

will vs. *be going to*

4 Complete the sentences with *be going to* for future plans and intentions, or *will* for predictions. Use the verbs in brackets.

1 I think more people _will recycle_ in the future. (recycle)
2 I _____ all my homework on Friday night before I go out. (do)
3 He's a very good footballer – I think he _____ for Brazil one day! (play)
4 We _____ petrol in cars in the future. (not use)
5 Danny and Sara _____ house in six months. (move)
6 We _____ the football tonight, we've got other plans. (not watch)

☐ Total: 5

Present continuous for future

5 **Write sentences with the present continuous about Jeannine's plans.**

1 *She's playing basketball at 5 o'clock on Monday.*
2 _____
3 _____
4 _____
5 _____
6 _____

Monday	play basketball at 5 o'clock
Tuesday	do Maths exam at 3 o'clock
Wednesday	go to Tom's party at 7 o'clock
Thursday	go to the cinema with Katrina at 8 o'clock
Friday	go swimming after school
Saturday	do yoga in the afternoon

Total: 5

Language builder

6 Circle **the correct options.**

Jake: I ¹_____ Japan on a student exchange.
Naomi: Really? I ²_____ to Japan last year. I had ³_____ time!
Jake: Can you give me ⁴_____advice? What ⁵_____ I take with me?
Naomi: Take a really good camera. I took ⁶_____ fantastic photos on my trip. ⁷_____ any Japanese?
Jake: I study Japanese at school. That's why I ⁸_____ on this trip. But I'm not as good as some of the others in my class.

1 **a** am going to visit
  b will visit
  c visit
2 **a** go
  b was going
  c went
3 **a** best
  b the best
  c the better
4 **a** much
  b any
  c many
5 **a** should
  b must
  c will
6 **a** some
  b any
  c much
7 **a** Are you speaking
  b Were you speaking
  c Do you speak
8 **a** go
  b am going
  c will go

Total: 7

Vocabulary builder

7 Circle **the correct options.**

1 We buy milk in _____ or glass bottles.
  a cartons   **b** paper bags   **c** glass jars
2 After lunch, my dad washed all the plates in the _____.
  a mirror   **b** sink   **c** desk
3 Does your _____ make photocopies?
  a printer   **b** memory stick   **c** tablet
4 For me, _____ is being with my friends.
  a illness   **b** kindness   **c** happiness
5 I enjoyed my job and I was _____ a lot of money.
  a selling   **b** earning   **c** shopping
6 I'd like to _____ children in the future.
  a make   **b** do   **c** have
7 I spend a lot of money _____ clothes.
  a to   **b** on   **c** for
8 Can you help me _____ the washing, please?
  a do   **b** make   **c** have
9 Before I go to university, I'll _____ a year out.
  a go   **b** be   **c** take
10 When I _____ , I want to be a photographer.
  a grow up   **b** am born   **c** get on
11 As soon as I'm eighteen, I'm going to _____ home.
  a go   **b** leave   **c** buy

Total: 10

Speaking

8 **Put the conversation in the correct order.**

1 ___ B: Absolutely. That's a much better idea.
2 ___ A: Do you think university students should get a weekend job?
3 ___ A: I suppose you're right. Do you think they should get a job in the holidays?
4 ___ B: Maybe, but I also think they need that time to study.

Total: 4

Total: 50

will vs. be going to

Remember that:
- we use **be going to** to talk about future plans and intentions.
  ✓ **I'm going to** study on Saturday night.
  ✗ ~~I will study on Saturday night.~~
- we use **will**, not be going to, to talk about predictions.
  ✓ If I can, I **will** call you tomorrow.
  ✗ ~~If I can, I'm going to call you tomorrow.~~

1 (Circle) the correct words.

✉ **New mail**

Hi Zara,
I'm glad you ¹ will / (are going to) come to the festival with us next weekend. Here are the plans – ² **we'll / we're going to** meet at the train station at 11.30 and ³ **we're going to / we'll** get a train at midday. There ⁴ **are going to / will** be lots of bands on in the afternoon and they probably ⁵ **aren't going to / won't** finish until around midnight. Do you think your dad ⁶ **will / is going to** pick us up if we ask him?
Thanks,
Lily

Present continuous for future

Remember that:
- we use the present continuous to talk about future plans and intentions.
  ✓ He**'s going** to Brazil on holiday this summer.
- we use the present simple to talk about facts, habits and routines.
  ✓ She **visits** her grandparents every summer.

2 Are the sentences correct? Correct the incorrect sentences.
1 At the weekend he is sleeping until 9 o'clock in the morning.
   At the weekend, he sleeps until 9 o'clock in
   the morning.
2 They are flying to Moscow next Wednesday.
   _____
3 John plays the piano in the school concert this year.
   _____
4 My friends have a party next Saturday.
   _____
5 He always travels to school by bus.
   _____

Verbs with prepositions

Remember, some verbs take a preposition between the verb and the indirect object. Don't forget the preposition!
   ✓ I enjoy **listening to** my mp3 player on the bus.
   ✗ ~~I enjoy listening my mp3 player on the bus.~~

3 Are the sentences correct? Add the correct preposition where necessary.
1 I will wait ^for you in front of the cinema.
2 They were listening the radio this morning.
3 If you haven't got any money, I will pay the tickets.
4 Young people often dream flying.
5 Do you spend a lot of money books?
6 I want to learn English on the Internet.

Time expressions

Remember that:
- we use **on** before dates and days of the week.
  ✓ I flew to Paris **on** 6 July.
- we use **in** before months, seasons and years.
  ✓ I went to Paris **in** July.
- we use **at** before the time.
  ✓ The plane landed **at** 6.45 pm.
- we don't usually use a preposition before **next/last/ this week/month/morning**, etc.
  ✓ I am going to Argentina **next summer**.
  ✗ ~~I am going to Argentina on next summer.~~

4 Correct five more mistakes in the dialogue.

Rory: Hi, Karen, what are you doing?
Karen: I'm going to the dentist ~~on~~ ^at 10 o'clock. Then, on this afternoon, I'm meeting Sarah to talk about our holiday. We're going to Italy with her parents on July!
Rory: Wow! That's exciting. What are you doing this evening?
Karen: I'm going to the cinema. The film begins on 8 o'clock. Do you want to come with us?
Rory: Oh, thank you, but I can't. I've got an exam at next week, so I have to study. The exam's on Tuesday. Maybe we can go to the cinema on next Saturday? I think there's usually a film at about 2 o'clock.
Karen: Great! See you there! Good luck with your exam.

7 Look out!

Vocabulary
Accidents and injuries

1 ★ **Find nine more verbs for accidents and injuries in the word search. Write them under the pictures.**

c	r	a	s	h	h	f	o	l	b
p	l	e	h	i	n	u	n	e	r
s	f	a	l	l	g	t	r	g	e
m	l	d	a	n	b	r	r	t	a
t	e	i	l	o	u	a	c	o	k
r	a	x	p	p	r	p	b	u	t
i	n	d	l	r	n	n	r	i	t
p	r	e	b	a	n	g	v	b	e

1 _hurt_
your back

2 _____
over the dog

3 _____
your car

4 _____
your finger

5 _____
your head

6 _____ off
your bike

7 _____ on
ice

8 _____
your leg

9 _____
your hand

10 _____
your fingers

2 ★★ **Complete the sentences with the past tense of the verbs from Exercise 1.**

1 When I was ten I ____*fell off*____ my bike and _____ my leg. I couldn't do sport for ages!
2 The man was really tall so he _____ his head when he went through the door.
3 The robber _____ over a dog when he was running away and dropped the woman's bag.
4 Someone _____ their car outside our school yesterday. Everyone heard the noise.
5 He _____ his hand when he was cooking a fried egg.
6 My granddad _____ on some ice when he was walking to the shops and _____ his back.
7 She _____ her finger when she was opening a can.

3 ★★ (Circle) **the wrong word.**

1 I banged my (car) / head / knee.
2 She **fell off / broke / hurt** her skateboard.
3 He **broke / hurt / tripped** his leg skiing.
4 You trapped your **foot / finger / chest**.
5 I **cut / fell / burnt** my finger yesterday.
6 He tripped over **the dog / your bike / the house**.

4 ★★★ **Complete the story with the correct form of the words in the box.**

> trip/over   fall off/bike   burn/hand
> cut/finger   ~~hurt/back~~   crash/car
> bang/head

Yesterday there were a lot of accidents in our house. My dad [1]_**hurt his back**_ when he tried to move the sofa. My mum [2]_____ when she opened a can of cat food and then later she [3]_____ while she was cooking some chicken. Then my granddad [4]_____ the cat and [5]_____ on the wall. My sister went cycling in the park and [6]_____ . She couldn't walk and her leg hurt, so we all went to the hospital in Dad's car. Then Dad [7]_____ into an ambulance! I was fine!

5 ★★★ **Do you know anyone who has a lot of accidents? Have your friends had an accident or injured themselves? Write at least five sentences.**

When Jamie was six, he fell off a wall and broke his arm.

Language focus 1

Present perfect

1 ★ **Complete the rules in the grammar table with the words in the box.**

> hasn't   has   when   have   haven't

1	We use the present perfect to talk about things in the past. We don't know exactly _____ they happened.
2	Affirmative: I/We/You/They _____ + past participle He/She/It _____ + past participle
3	Negative: I/We/You/They _____ + past participle He/She/It _____ + past participle

2 ★★ **Write the past participle of the verbs in the table.**

crash	ride
1 _crashed_	**2** _____
fall	teach
3 _____	**4** _____
meet	break
5 _____	**6** _____
slip	go
7 _____	**8** _____

3 ★★ **Complete the sentences with the present perfect form of the verbs from Exercise 2.**

1 Jackie _hasn't met_ a famous person. (✗)
2 I _____ my arm twice in the same place! (✓)
3 They _____ to hospital ten times! (✓)
4 We _____ a motorbike but we want to! (✗)
5 Fred _____ his car, but he's OK. (✓)
6 She _____ on some ice in the street. (✓)
7 You _____ off your bike today. You're getting better! (✗)
8 My English teacher _____ at this school for very long. (✗)

4 ★★ **Complete the text with the present perfect form of the verbs in brackets.**

My friends and I did an internet quiz called *50 things to do before you're 18*. All of us ¹ _have been_ (go) camping but we ² _____ (not have) a holiday without adults. We ³ _____ (watch) a film in 3D. We ⁴ _____ (not meet) a famous person, but I ⁵ _____ (see) Penelope Cruz in the street. David ⁶ _____ (hold) a snake at a safari park, and Alicia ⁷ _____ (sing) in a concert – actually, lots of concerts! We ⁸ _____ (not do) anything dangerous like bungee jumping. But we're only 15 so there's lots of time!

5 ★★★ **Write sentences about what Candice has and hasn't done.**

crash her bike	do something dangerous	break her leg	meet someone famous	ride a horse
✓	✓	✗	✗	✓

1 _She has crashed her bike._
2 _____
3 _____
4 _____
5 _____

Explore expressions with *get*

6 ★★ **Match the sentence beginnings (1–6) with the sentence endings (a–f).**

1 Yesterday I missed the bus and got ___ _e_
2 I'm sorry you're not feeling well and I hope you get ___
3 I've never slipped on ice and got ___
4 If I go home late, my mum gets ___
5 I hate sitting in the back of the car because I always get ___
6 Do you know anyone who doesn't want to get ___

a injured.
b married?
c better soon.

d sick.
e home late.
f worried.

Listening and vocabulary

The body

1 ★★ **Use the picture to complete the crossword.**

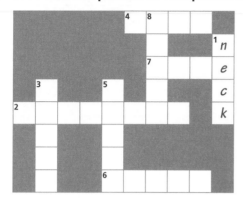

2 ★★★ **Write the correct parts of the body from Exercise 1.**

1 You shouldn't put these on the table while you're eating. _elbows_
2 This is always behind you. _____
3 You cannot break this. _____
4 This is where you put your watch. _____
5 You use this to move your head. _____
6 Hang your school bag from these. _____
7 When you fall over you usually hurt these. _____
8 Your socks help to keep these warm. _____

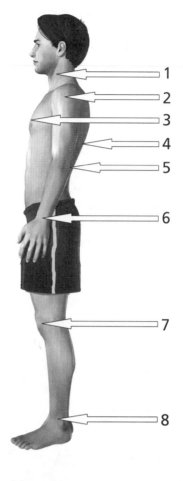

Listening

3 ★★ 🔊 07 **Listen to Sophie talking to her friend Rob about extreme sports. Tick (✓) the sports that Sophie has done.**

canyoning

parkour

bungee jumping

hang-gliding

canyoning	✓	climbing	☐
football	☐	hang-gliding	☐
kite-surfing	☐	parkour	☐
rafting	☐	running	☐
snowboarding	☐	tennis	☐
volleyball	☐	windsurfing	☐

4 ★★ 🔊 07 **Listen again and choose the correct options.**

1 What does Sophie say about canyoning?
   ⓐ It's dangerous.
   b She's tried it once.
   c She's had an accident.
2 Sophie explains that …
   a she likes being scared.
   b she never gets frightened.
   c she doesn't take risks.
3 Rob says that he …
   a hasn't done any sport.
   b likes being scared too.
   c enjoys safer sports.
4 Sophie hasn't been bungee jumping because …
   a her parents think it's too expensive.
   b she isn't old enough.
   c she prefers other sports.
5 Sophie explains that parkour …
   a is only practised in France.
   b isn't very difficult.
   c is a sport you do in a city.
6 What is true about Sophie?
   a She's fallen off her bike.
   b She's broken her shoulder.
   c She's crashed her surfboard.

Language focus 2

Present perfect: questions

1 ⭐ **Circle the correct words in the grammar table.**

1	We use questions in the present perfect to ask about **present / past** experiences.
2	**Have / Has** you ever **be / been** to Spain? **Have / Has** your brother **started / start** university?
3	To ask about your **whole life / recent experiences** put *ever* **before / after** the subject.
4	Have they **ever tried / tried ever** bungee jumping? Yes, they **has / have**.

2 ⭐⭐ **Write questions with the present perfect. Then match the questions to the answers.**

1 Jack / go / kite-surfing?
Has Jack been kite-surfing?   b

2 it / snow / a lot?
_____   __

3 your parents / crash / their car / ever / ?
_____   __

4 Helen / cut / her hand?
_____   __

5 we / see / this film about a plane crash / ever / ?
_____   __

6 you / break / your arm / ever / ?
_____   __

a Yes, I have. Twice!
b No, he hasn't.
c No, they haven't.
d Yes, we have. Last month!
e Yes, she has. In Art class.
f Yes, it has. Look out for ice!

3 ⭐⭐⭐ **Write questions in the present perfect for these answers.**

1 *Have you ever broken a part of your body?*
Yes, I have. I broke my leg last year.

2 _____
No, I haven't but I'd like to visit Rio.

3 _____
Yes, I have. I went to see Beyoncé last October.

4 _____
I'm not sure. I think I've read about 30 books in my life.

5 _____
Yes, I have. I fell off my bike once and hurt my leg.

6 _____
Yes, we have. We had a cat a few years ago.

Past simple vs. present perfect

4 ⭐⭐ **Complete the sentences with the correct form of the past simple or present perfect and the verbs in brackets.**

1 I ___*fell off*___ my bike yesterday and hurt my arm. (fall off)

2 My brother _____ his leg three times. He loves dangerous sports. (break)

3 I've eaten rabbit but I _____ horse. (eat)

4 My sister _____ married in 2010. (get)

5 I _____ snowboarding with my family in December. (go)

6 My best friend _____ a new tablet. It's amazing! (buy)

7 I _____ at 7 am this morning. (get up)

8 They _____ to New York but we haven't. (go)

Explore compound nouns

5 ⭐ **Match the parts of the compound words.**

1 forest ――――――― **a** life
2 charity ――――――― **b** floor
3 fire   **c** worker
4 fishing   **d** wood
5 wild   **e** boat

6 ⭐⭐ **Complete the sentences with the words in Exercise 5.**

1 I've always wanted to be a *charity worker* to help other people.

2 My uncle has a _____ and we sometimes go on the lake in it.

3 We'll need lots of _____ to keep warm when we go camping.

4 I love watching TV programmes about _____ – especially about African animals.

5 In the morning, we saw some rabbits running across the _____ .

Reading

1 ★ **Read the text about a town in Canada. What is Churchill trying to do about polar bears?**

POLAR BEAR ALERT

Churchill, on Hudson Bay in Manitoba, Northern Canada, is the polar bear capital of the world. The town has about 800 *inhabitants* and close by there are about the same number of bears!

The town of Churchill and the bears lived together peacefully for 300 years with only two fatal bear attacks. However, climate change has made *co-existence* more difficult. The ice *season* in Hudson Bay has got shorter, and this has made it difficult for them to find food in spring and autumn. So, many bears are *starving* and coming to look for food in Churchill. Recently a bear injured two people at night.

Churchill wants bears and humans to co-exist, so it has a Polar Bear *Alert* programme, managed by Bob Wilson of Manitoba Conservation. The idea is not to kill the bears, but to make them scared of people so they run away. Bob has different ways to scare the bears: a pistol with blanks, a noisy air horn, firecrackers, even a paintball gun! There is also a special bear 'jail' if they don't run away. Then, Manitoba Conservation takes these bears back into the tundra by helicopter.

Bob and his colleagues patrol Churchill 24-hours a day. In November, one of the most dangerous months, there are often 20 alerts a day. Luckily, most *encounters* between people and bears in Churchill haven't been serious. One woman threw a bag of shopping at a bear to scare it away. Last year, there were more than 160 similar incidents in one week.

Most of the bears are sub-adult males. 'Teenagers,' said one officer. 'They're the ones that get into trouble.'

2 ★★ **Match the words in bold in the text with the definitions.**

1 Summer, winter, spring or autumn. _season_
2 When different people or things live together. _____
3 A warning to tell people something dangerous might happen. _____
4 When a person or animal is very hungry because there is no food to eat. _____
5 The people who live in a place. _____
6 When people or animals meet by chance. _____

3 ★★ **Read the text again and answer the questions.**

1 How many polar bears live near Churchill?
   About 800.
2 What is the effect of climate change on the people and bears?
   _____
3 Have they attacked anyone in the town recently?
   _____
4 What does the Polar Bear Alert programme try to do?
   _____
5 What does Bob use to frighten the bears?
   _____
6 What do they do with bears that don't leave the town?
   _____

4 **Write three or four questions to ask Bob Wilson or one of the people who saw a bear in the town. Then write the answers – you can invent them!**

   _____
   _____
   _____
   _____

Writing

An email refusing an invitation

1 **Read Edward's email. Why can't he go camping?**

✉ *Your* MAIL   ⊕ New   Reply | ▾   Delete   Junk | ▾

Hi George,

Thanks for writing to me about the camping trip next weekend. I'm sorry, I'd love to go with you but I can't. My cousin's getting married that weekend. I didn't tell you before because I completely forgot about it. My mum told me months ago and I put it in my phone, but then I lost the phone!

He's going to have the party on the beach. I've never been to a beach party before so it'll be fun. All my cousins are going to be there. I haven't seen them since last summer. So how about another weekend?

Sorry again! If you can't change the dates, have a great time. I'll send you some photos of the party.

Enjoy yourselves!

Edward

2 **Read Edward's email again. Answer the questions.**

1 When did Edward's mum tell him about the party? _____
2 Why did Edward forget about it? _____
3 Where is the party going to be? _____
4 When did Edward last see his cousins? _____
5 What will he send George? _____

Useful language Polite language for refusing ——————

3 **Find expressions in Edward's email with the same meaning as the sentences below.**

1 Sorry, I can't come.
   I'm sorry, I'd love to go with you but I can't.
2 Have fun.
   _____
3 I'm really sorry.
   _____
4 Could we go another weekend?
   _____

4 **Put the words in order to make sentences that explain why you need to refuse an invitation.**

1 hurt / leg / fell / I / and / my
   I fell and hurt my leg.
2 party / are / My / having / a / cousins
   _____
3 Monday / I / an / have to / on / study / exam / for
   _____
4 bike / arm / fell off / my / my / I / broke / and
   _____
5 70th / and / surprise party / birthday / we're / my / having / It's / a / grandmother's
   _____

5 **Some verbs in English have two objects. Rewrite the sentences so the direct object in the first sentence comes at the end of the new sentence.**

1 My parents bought a present for me.
   My parents bought me a present.
2 Helen showed the photos of the party to me.
   _____
3 We gave a surprise to my dad.
   _____
4 Jeff sent the video to me.
   _____
5 Aidan lent his bike to me for the weekend.
   _____
6 My mum found some tickets for me.
   _____

Writing

> **WRITING TIP**
> Make it better! ✓ ✓ ✓
> Finish the email by telling your friends to have a good time.
> *I hope you have a great time at the concert.*

6 Which sentence does <u>not</u> tell someone to have a good time?
  1 Enjoy yourselves!
  2 I'm sorry I'm going to miss it.
  3 I hope you have a great time.
  4 I hope you like the camp.
  5 Have a great weekend!

7 Write the information in the order it is in Edward's email.

  apologise again
  close the email
  say why you can't go to the event
  suggest another time to meet
  ~~apologise~~

  1 *apologise*   4 _____
  2 _____   5 _____
  3 _____

PLAN

8 You are going to write an email refusing an invitation to a friend or family member. Use the ideas below to help you. Then make notes.
You've been invited to …

  a family party   a concert   the cinema   a party

You can't go because …

  you/your friend had an accident
  you haven't got enough money
  you are busy that day

WRITE

9 Write the email. Look at page 83 of the Student's Book to help you.

  _____
  _____
  _____
  _____
  _____
  _____
  _____
  _____
  _____
  _____
  _____
  _____

CHECK

10 Check your writing. Can you say YES to these questions?
  • Did you use the ideas in Exercise 8?
  • Did you use polite language for refusing the invitation?
  • Did you explain why you can't go?
  • Did you use verbs with two objects correctly?
  • Did you tell your friends to have a good time?
  • Did you write the information in your email in the correct order?

Do you need to write a second draft?

Vocabulary
Accidents and injuries

1 **Match the sentence halves.**

1 I hurt … _b_
2 I burnt … ___
3 I cut … ___
4 I slipped … ___
5 I broke … ___
6 I banged … ___
7 I tripped … ___

a my finger on that big knife.
b my back while I was lifting some boxes.
c my hand while I was cooking.
d my head on the table.
e my leg when I fell off my bike.
f over the dog when I was running into the kitchen.
g on the ice while I was skating.

Total: 6

The body

2 **Write the name for each part of the body.**

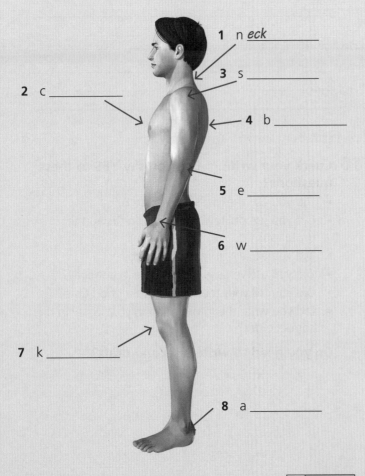

1 n _eck_
3 s _____
2 c _____
4 b _____
5 e _____
6 w _____
7 k _____
8 a _____

Total: 7

Language focus
Present perfect: affirmative and negative

3 **Complete the email with the present perfect form of the verbs in brackets.**

Hi Julie,
We're having fun on holiday. My parents love climbing but we ¹ _haven't climbed_ (not climb) any hills because mum ² _____ (hurt) her ankle and can't walk very well!
We ³ _____ (go) to the beach, and I ⁴ _____ (have) some surfing lessons.
My sister ⁵ _____ (try) ten different flavours of ice cream. How about you? How was your holiday?
Tania

Total: 4

Present perfect: questions

4 **Put the words in order to make questions. Use the past participle form of the verbs in brackets.**

1 ever / you / (write) / a diary / Have
   Have you ever written a diary ?
2 ever / your brother / Has / a competition / (win)
   _____ ?
3 (eat) / ever / you / shark / Have
   _____ ?
4 you / Have / (break) / ever / your ankle
   _____ ?
5 Have / your parents / (visit) / Australia / ever
   _____ ?
6 your sister / in a concert / (play) / Has / violin / ever
   _____ ?

Total: 5

Past simple vs. present perfect

5 **Circle the correct options.**

1 Barak Obama **has become / became** the US president in 2009.
2 **Has your country ever had / Did your country ever have** a woman president?
3 Astronauts Neil Armstrong and Buzz Aldrin **have walked / walked** on the moon in July 1969.
4 The Wright brothers **have invented / invented** the world's first aeroplane.
5 Around 40% of Americans **travelled / have travelled** to another country.

Total: 4

Language builder

6 (Circle) the correct options to complete the conversation.

Liz:	Have you ever ¹_____ any bones?
Jamie:	Yes, I ²_____ my arm when I ³_____ skiing in Italy last winter.
Liz:	That's terrible! ⁴_____ it really painful?
Jamie:	Yes! I ⁵_____ use my arm for about three months.
Liz:	I ⁶_____ skiing this winter. I hope I don't have an accident! What ⁷_____ I wear?
Jamie:	You ⁸_____ wear a helmet. That's very important, and you ⁹_____ ski on your own.
Liz:	That's good advice. Do you think snowboarding is ¹⁰_____ than skiing?
Jamie:	Skiing is ¹¹_____ than snowboarding because you can turn more quickly.

1. **a** break   **b** broke   **(c)** broken
2. **a** break   **b** broke   **c** broken
3. **a** was   **b** have   **c** were
4. **a** Did   **b** Was   **c** Were
5. **a** couldn't   **b** shouldn't   **c** haven't
6. **a** will go   **b** am going to go
    c go
7. **a** will   **b** should   **c** could
8. **a** should   **b** could   **c** must
9. **a** mustn't   **b** couldn't   **c** won't
10. **a** most dangerous   **b** more dangerous
    c dangerous
11. **a** less dangerous   **b** the least dangerous
    c dangerous

Total: 10

Vocabulary builder

7 (Circle) the correct options.
1. Have you ever _____ your car?
    a hurt   **b** slipped   **(c)** crashed
2. Tom fell off his bike and _____ injured.
    a did   **b** got   **c** turned
3. You haven't written _____ the new words.
    a on   **b** down   **c** for
4. Why did you _____ your towel at me?
    a catch   **b** jump   **c** throw
5. I can't hear you. _____ the music!
    a Turn down   **b** Turn up   **c** Shut down

6. My mum _____ on ice and hurt her ankle.
    a banged   **b** tripped   **c** slipped
7. We haven't put the books in cardboard _____.
    a packets   **b** bags   **c** boxes
8. My brother was sick last week but he's getting _____.
    a better   **b** good   **c** home
9. She was very _____ because she didn't cry when she broke her wrist.
    a funny   **b** brave   **c** kind
10. Go _____ or you'll fall off your bike.
    a well   **b** quietly   **c** slowly

Total: 9

Speaking

8 **Complete the conversations with words from the box.**

terrible   no   ~~up~~   shame   sorry   How

1. **A:** Hi, Caroline!
    B: Hi Sam, what have you been _____*up*_____ to?
2. **A:** I hurt my finger.
    B: What a _____ !
3. **A:** I've burned my wrist.
    B: That's _____ .
4. **A:** Someone stole my bicycle!
    B: I'm _____ to hear that.
5. **A:** I've passed all my exams!
    B: _____ amazing!
6. **A:** I've hurt my hand.
    B: Oh _____ !

Total: 5

Total: 50

Present perfect

Remember that:

- we use subject + **have** + past participle to talk about past experiences. Don't forget to use **have**!
  - ✓ He can't play football because he **has** broken his leg.
  - ✗ ~~He can't play football because he broken his leg.~~
- we use **have** + subject + past participle to ask questions about past experiences.
  - ✓ **Has** he broken his leg?
  - ✗ ~~He has broken his leg?~~

1 Find and correct seven more mistakes in the email.

 New mail

Hi Tim,

I can't come to the picnic this afternoon! My dad can't drive me to the park because he ^has^ hurt his back. My brother can't bring me because he injured his foot. My sister fell off her bike and she thinks she broken her arm. And I have to stay at home because my dog eaten something bad. As for Martin, I not heard from him. You have seen him this week? I hope he not had an accident too!

ever or never?

Remember that:

- we can use **ever** or **never** to talk about experiences in the past.
- we use have + subject + **ever** + past participle to make questions.
  - ✓ Have you **ever** eaten fried insects?
  - ✗ ~~You have ever eaten fried insects?~~
- we use **ever**, not **never**, in statements after superlative adjectives.
  - ✓ It's the most serious accident he has **ever** had.
  - ✗ ~~It's the most serious accident he has never had.~~
- we do not use **never** in sentences that are already negative.
  - ✓ They have **never** been to Asia.
  - ✓ They haven't **ever** been to Asia.
  - ✗ ~~They haven't never been to Asia.~~

2 Are the sentences correct? Correct the incorrect sentences.

1 I never have been to Australia.
   I have never been to Australia.

2 It was the best party I have never been to.
   _____

3 You have ever travelled on an aeroplane?
   _____

4 This smartphone is the best phone I have ever had.
   _____

5 He's had a lot of accidents, but he hasn't never broken any bones.
   _____

6 He told us he has ever spoken English outside class.
   _____

7 Have they never been in hospital?
   _____

Spell it right! Past participles

Remember that:

- with irregular verbs, the past simple form of the verb and the past participle are often different. Look at the irregular verb table on page 127 of the Student's Book.
  - ✓ John **fell** (past simple) off his bike last week.
  - ✓ Come quickly! John **has fallen** (past participle) off his bike.

3 Write the correct past simple and past participle form of the verbs.

Infinitive	Past simple	Past participle
eat	_ate_	_eaten_
see	_____	_____
swim	_____	_____
fly	_____	_____
sing	_____	_____
write	_____	_____
speak	_____	_____
break	_____	_____
fall	_____	_____
have	_____	_____
take	_____	_____

8 Having fun

Vocabulary

Free time activities

1 ★ **Complete the free time activities with the verbs in the box.**

> take watch spend draw play
> ~~have~~ meet play use read

1 ___have___ a party
2 _____ computer games
3 _____ books or magazines
4 _____ friends
5 _____ films
6 _____ time with your family
7 _____ an instrument
8 _____ the Internet
9 _____ pictures
10 _____ photos

2 ★★ **Choose the correct options.**

1 Let's stay at home and (watch) / use films.
2 At weekends, I go to the shopping centre to **meet / take** my friends.
3 If you're bored, you can **use / draw** pictures.
4 My dad likes **reading / using** the Internet to find information.
5 My sister **took / spent** some photos at the zoo.
6 **Having / Reading** books and magazines is a nice way to relax.
7 Barry's **using / having** a party on Friday for his birthday.

3 ★★ **Complete the sentences with the correct form of the verbs in Exercise 1.**

1 Yesterday I ____met____ my friends in the park.
2 While I _____ the Internet, my mum called me for dinner.
3 I _____ (not) an instrument, but I'd like to learn the guitar.
4 It was raining so we stayed at home and _____ computer games.
5 My friend Lucy always _____ pictures in class.
6 I don't really like _____ books or magazines.
7 It was my dad's birthday so we _____ a party.
8 _____ you _____ a lot of photos while you were on holiday?
9 I think it's important to _____ time with your family at the weekend.
10 When I don't want to go out, I stay at home and _____ films on my computer.

4 ★★★ **Which free time activity are they talking about? Write a sentence.**

1 'This is a good one of you and Paul, you're both smiling. I'm going to put it on my blog.'
  She took a photo.
2 'I've only got about 20 more pages to read. I can't wait to see what happens!'
  She _____
3 'Let's make it a surprise. Don't tell her. We'll invite all her friends.'
  They _____
4 'I've got a new one. It's cool but I'm only on Level 5 and there are 100 levels!'
  He _____
5 'OK, 11 o'clock at the door of the sports centre. Don't be late.'
  They _____
6 'I like chatting with my cousins and my mum and dad always have a great time.'
  She _____
7 'We saw a really good one last night about Sherlock Holmes, the detective.'
  They _____

Language focus 1

one/ones

1 ★ **Complete the rules in the grammar table with the words in the box.**

> one   noun   one   ones   ones

1	We can use *one* or *ones* when we don't want to repeat a _____ in a sentence.
2	We use _____ to replace a singular noun.
3	My brother loves these cakes, especially this _____ with white chocolate.
4	We use _____ to replace a plural noun.
5	You can buy these flowers for Mum and I'll buy those _____ for Auntie Sue.

2 ★★ **Cross out the repeated words in each sentence. Write *one* or *ones* to replace them.**

1 **A:** Can I have a cake, please?
 B: Which ~~cake~~ *one* would you like, chocolate or strawberry?

2 I love the photos of the party, especially the photos of us dancing!

3 I don't want a small wedding. I want a big wedding!

4 **A:** Can you pass me my jacket?
 B: Which jacket is it?
 A: The black jacket with a grey hood.

5 **A:** Do you want a glass of water?
 B: No, I've got a glass of water, thanks.

Indefinite pronouns

3 ★ **Complete the rules in the grammar table with the words in the box.**

> negative   places   people   affirmative   things

1	We use *someone/no one/everyone/anyone* to talk about _____ .
2	We use *something/nothing/everything/anything* to talk about _____ .
3	We use *somewhere/nowhere/everywhere/anywhere* to talk about _____ .
4	We use the pronouns starting with *some-* and *every-* in _____ sentences.
5	We use the pronouns starting with *no-* and *any-* in _____ sentences. *I haven't got anything to do.* *I've got nothing to do.*

4 ★★ **Complete the conversation with *some*, *any*, *no* or *every*.**

Mum: Joe, have you seen the cat? I've looked [1] _*every*_ where, but I can't find him.

Joe: No, I haven't! I haven't seen him [2] _____ where this morning.

Mum: What's wrong?

Joe: I'm bored! There's [3] _____ thing exciting to do in this place. I've got [4] _____ where to go and [5] _____ one to go out with.

Mum: Why not? Where are all your friends?

Joe: [6] _____ one's busy today. Gary's gone [7] _____ where with his parents, Josh's grandparents are visiting him, and I can't do [8] _____ thing with Kyle because he's ill.

Mum: Well, help me find the cat, then!

Joe: OK, but wait a minute. [9] _____ one's texting me. Maybe Gary's back home!

5 ★★★ **Rewrite the sentences with the words in brackets.**

1 All the students arrived in time for school. (arrive / late / for school)
 Nobody arrived late for school.

2 We haven't got any food. (There's / to eat)
 _____

3 All the shops are closed. (There's / to go shopping)
 _____

4 All the people I know live in flats. (live / house)
 _____

5 There's no noise. (can't / hear)
 _____

Explore expressions with *have*

6 ★★ **Match the sentence beginnings (1–6) with the sentence endings (a–f).**

1 At the end of the school year, we had   _b_
2 I wasn't having   ___
3 When I get up in the morning, I always have   ___
4 On Sunday, we went out for lunch and had   ___
5 I know that if I ever have   ___
6 While we were cycling up the hill, I had a   ___

a a shower and get dressed for school.
b a party with everyone in our class.
c rest because I was very tired.
d a meal in an Indian restaurant.
e a problem, I can talk to my parents.
f a good time so I decided to go home.

Listening and vocabulary

Adjectives of feeling

1 ⭐ **Find eight more adjectives of feeling in the word search.**

t	i	r	e	d	g	d	t	i	i
r	h	b	m	v	y	r	e	l	n
b	m	e	b	o	u	p	s	e	t
a	f	r	a	i	d	f	u	x	e
v	g	e	r	a	s	d	r	c	r
a	n	g	r	y	g	f	p	i	e
b	t	e	a	w	k	l	r	t	s
z	o	r	s	r	e	j	i	e	t
n	y	r	s	e	w	r	s	d	e
b	o	r	e	d	t	t	e	h	d
e	e	r	d	q	d	c	d	g	k

2 ⭐⭐ **Complete the sentences with the adjectives from Exercise 1.**

1 I didn't know you were ___afraid___ of dogs. It's OK, he won't bite!
2 I played tennis for two hours. Now I'm feeling very _____ .
3 Steve can't come to my party. I'm quite _____ , I really wanted to see him.
4 Oh no, not another romantic comedy film! I'm really _____ of them. The story is always the same.
5 I was walking to school and I slipped on some ice in front of all my classmates. I was really _____ .
6 We're going to an amusement park tomorrow. I'm very _____ . I love them!
7 I can't believe Caroline can play three instruments. I'm really _____ .
8 Alan borrowed €20 from me and he hasn't paid me back. I'm really _____ with him.
9 My dad loves reading about science. He's really _____ in it.

Listening

3 ⭐⭐ 🔊 **08 Listen to Grace and Karla talking about April Fool's Day. What happened in their class?**

4 ⭐⭐⭐ 🔊 **08 Circle the correct option.**
1 They played a joke on their **biology** / history teacher.
2 They looked **in books / on the Internet** for April Fool's jokes.
3 They made it look like there was a murder in **the classroom / the main hall**.
4 They prepared it at **lunch time / break time**.
5 They waited for the teacher to **come in / leave the classroom**.
6 The teacher looked **worried / angry**.
7 The teacher **told / didn't tell** the class an April Fool's joke.

Language focus 2

too + adjective

1 ★ (Circle) **the correct words in the grammar table.**

We use *too* + adjective when we want to say something is ¹**more / less** than we want or need it to be. Its meaning is usually ²**affirmative / negative**.

2 ★★ **Put the words in order to make sentences.**

1 her / too / I / talk / to / was / to / embarrassed
I was too embarrassed to talk to her.

2 surprised / anything / Noel / say / was / too / to
_____

3 me / call / was / too / to / upset / Adam
_____

4 is / to / bag / too / carry / This / heavy
_____

5 says / get married / young / I'm / mum / too / My / to
_____

6 small / too / everything / is / cardboard box / to / carry / This
_____
_____

(not) adjective + *enough*

3 ★ (Circle) **the correct words in the grammar table.**

Enough always comes ¹**before / after** an adjective. We use it to say that we have ²**less than / as much as / more than** we want or need.

4 ★★ **Complete the sentences with the adjectives in the box.**

warm   cool   tall   ~~old~~   fast   strong

1 I'm not ____*old*____ enough to learn to drive. I'm only 13.

2 This plastic bag is not _____ enough to hold all these vegetables.

3 Do you think the tea is _____ enough to drink now?

4 I hate my computer! It's not _____ enough to play videos on the Internet.

5 If the room is not _____ enough, I can give you a blanket.

6 Am I _____ enough to play basketball?

5 ★★★ **Rewrite the sentences with the opposite adjectives and *too* or *enough*.**

1 You were too late to see the start of the football match.
You weren't early enough to see the start of the football match.

2 This work is too bad to pass the exam.
_____

3 My flat isn't big enough for a party.
_____

4 We're too young to watch this film.
_____

5 He was too weak to hold the books.
_____

(E)xplore making nouns from verbs

6 ★★ **Complete the second sentence so it has a similar meaning to the first.**

1 It's easy to send photos with this mobile phone.
____*Sending*____ photos is easy with this mobile phone.

2 It's great fun to go to the park.
_____ to the park is great fun.

3 It's better to swim in the sea than in a pool.
_____ in the sea is better than in a pool.

4 I feel excited when I go out on Friday nights.
_____ out on Friday nights makes me feel excited.

5 It feels great to have a shower after doing sport.
_____ a shower after doing sport feels great.

Reading

1 ★ **Read the text about different amusement parks. Which has one of the highest roller coasters in the world?**

A fun day out

The first amusement parks opened in the USA in the 1870s, and the first **roller coaster** appeared in 1884. Now amusement parks are popular all over the world, but they're not all the same. Here are a few examples from different parts of the world.

Crocosaurus Cove, Darwin, Australia

This **aquarium** and theme park has big and small crocodiles and you can stand very close to them. There are lots of other attractions, too. You can have your photo taken with a baby "croc" or you can feed the snakes and crocodiles.

Universal Studios, Singapore

This theme park is small but exciting! For many people the best **ride** in the park is the *Transformers*. Visitors sit in a small car and go on a fantastic 3D **battle**. Modern technology creates some very real fire, water and smoke effects. For people who don't like rides, there's also the beach, an aquarium and other attractions based on popular films.

Window of the World, Shenzhen, China

This theme park has **replicas** of 130 famous **monuments** from around the world, including the Eiffel Tower (one third of the size of the real one), the Pyramids of Giza, the Coliseum in Rome, Niagara Falls and the Grand Canyon! There are also cultural events from around the world, and indoor water and ski parks.

Six Flags Magic Mountain, California

This amusement park is famous for its roller coasters! It has 18, the most in the world, including one of the tallest in the world! But if you're afraid of roller coasters, Six Flags also has themed areas with concerts, shows, games and over a hundred other rides. It's very near Hollywood so it has appeared in a lot of famous films and TV series. Some of the rides are themed, e.g. *Batman*, *Superman: escape from Krypton* and others.

2 ★★ **Complete the definitions with the words in bold in the text.**
1 A ___replica___ is a copy of something.
2 A _____ is a very fast, small train at an amusement park.
3 A machine in an amusement park that people go on is called a _____.
4 A _____ is an important building or place that many people know or have visited.
5 An _____ is a place where you go to see fish and other sea animals.
6 A fight between two groups of people is a _____.

3 ★★ **Read the text again. Match the parks with the sentences. Write *CC* for Crocosaurus Cove, *U* for Universal, *WW* for Window on the World, and *SF* for Six Flags.**
1 _U_ has a ride with great special effects.
2 ___ has very dangerous animals.
3 ___ has the world record for something.
4 ___ includes attractions for people who like cinema.
5 ___ takes you on a type of international tour.
6 ___ has animals you can see or touch.
7 ___ has a place where you can go swimming.

4 ★★ **Have you or your friends been to an amusement park? What did you do there? Write at least five sentences.**

_____
_____
_____
_____
_____
_____
_____
_____
_____

Writing

An email invitation to a friend

1 Read Andy's email. What is he going to do on his birthday and where is he going to do it?

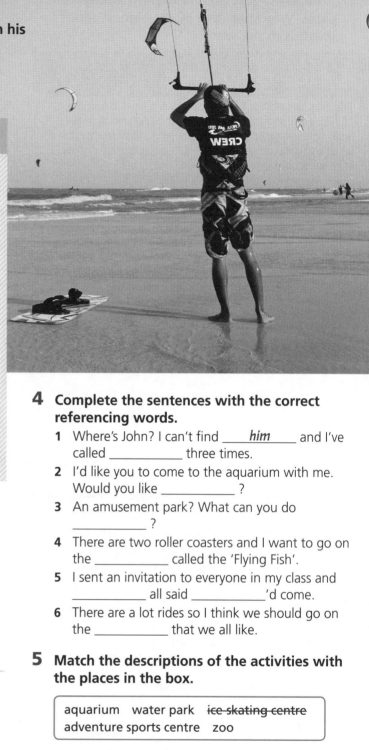

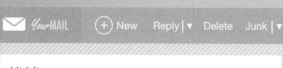

> Hi Nina,
>
> I haven't heard from you for ages. How are things at your new school? Is ¹**it** strict?
>
> I'm writing to invite you to my birthday party! I didn't want a big ²**one** so Mum suggested a day out with a few friends. I've decided to try a new sport called power kiting. Have you heard of ³**it**? It's a combination of skateboarding (I know you love ⁴**that** ☺) and flying a kite. What do you think?
>
> Anyway, ⁵**it**'s on Saturday 16 May. Martin and Alex are coming. We're meeting at my house at 10.30 am to go together. There's a fast food restaurant next to the beach, so we can have lunch ⁶**there**. Hope you can come!
>
> Write back soon,
> Andy

2 Read the email again. Answer the questions.
1 What does Andy invite Nina to?
2 What is power kiting?
3 When is he going power kiting?
4 Who is going with him?
5 Where are they meeting?
6 Where are they going to have lunch?

Useful language Referencing words ——

3 Look back at Andy's email. What do the words in **bold** (1–6) refer to?
1 *Nina's new school*
2 _____
3 _____
4 _____
5 _____
6 _____

4 Complete the sentences with the correct referencing words.
1 Where's John? I can't find ___*him*___ and I've called _____ three times.
2 I'd like you to come to the aquarium with me. Would you like _____ ?
3 An amusement park? What can you do _____ ?
4 There are two roller coasters and I want to go on the _____ called the 'Flying Fish'.
5 I sent an invitation to everyone in my class and _____ all said _____'d come.
6 There are a lot rides so I think we should go on the _____ that we all like.

5 Match the descriptions of the activities with the places in the box.

> aquarium   water park   ~~ice-skating centre~~
> adventure sports centre   zoo

1 It'll be cold and you'll need warm socks for the skates.   *ice-skating centre*
2 They're going to tell us about the animals and we can feed some of the birds.   _____
3 I don't think they'll let us swim with the dolphins but we can touch them.   _____
4 We're going to go down some huge water slides. Bring a towel!   _____
5 We can go on the climbing wall and go power kiting too.   _____

Writing

6 **Complete the sentences with the present continuous form of the verbs in brackets.**

1 We*'re meeting* (meet) at Gina's house at 2 o'clock.

2 Tom and I _____ (have) lunch at the water park.

3 We _____ (take) the bus to the zoo from the city centre.

4 Patricia and Nicola _____ (come) and we _____ (go) skating.

5 Jan and I _____ (leave) at 3 o'clock so let's meet at the door.

> **WRITING TIP**
>
> Make it better! ✓ ✓ ✓
> Finish your email invitation by saying how excited you are that your friend will come.
> *I'm really looking forward to seeing you.*

7 **Which sentence does <u>not</u> say that you are excited?**

1 Hope you can come!

2 It'll be great if you can come too!

3 I'm sure we'll have a fantastic time together!

4 I'm not sure what we're going to do.

5 I really hope you can join us.

8 **Order the things Andy does in his email (1–6).**

> finishes the email
> gives the reason for the celebration
> explains arrangements
> invites Nina
> ~~asks Nina about her life~~
> explains the activity

1 *asks Nina about her life*

2 _____

3 _____

4 _____

5 _____

6 _____

PLAN

9 **You are going to write an email to a friend inviting them to a day out on your birthday. Choose one of the ideas below or your own. Then use the information in Exercise 8 and make notes.**

a An ice-skating centre

b A water park

c An adventure sports centre

WRITE

10 **Write the email invitation. Look at page 93 of the Student's Book to help you.**

_____
_____
_____
_____
_____
_____
_____
_____
_____
_____
_____
_____

CHECK

11 **Check your writing. Can you say YES to these questions?**

• Did you use the ideas in Exercise 8?

• Did you use referencing words correctly?

• Did you give a description of the activities?

• Did you talk about arrangements you've made with other people?

• Did you say you are excited about the plans?

Do you need to write a second draft?

Vocabulary

Free time activities

1 Match the verbs (1–10) and the nouns (a–j).

1	spend	a	an instrument
2	play	b	the Internet
3	read	c	a party
4	use	d	computer games
5	meet	e	photos
6	play	f	films
7	have	g	books or magazines
8	draw	h	time with your family
9	take	i	friends
10	watch	j	pictures

Total: 9

Adjectives of feeling

2 Match the sentence halves.

1 I'm angry …   _i_
2 I'm excited …   ___
3 I'm afraid …   ___
4 I'm upset …   ___
5 I'm embarrassed …   ___
6 I'm bored …   ___
7 I'm tired …   ___
8 I'm interested …   ___
9 I'm surprised …   ___

a because the teacher told everyone I didn't do my homework.
b of spiders. I hate them!
c because I couldn't sleep last night.
d in learning how to speak Chinese.
e because my best friend is moving away.
f about going to the ballet this weekend.
g that my grandmother is on Facebook!
h with these computer games. They're all the same.
i with my sister. She broke my mobile phone!

Total: 8

Language focus

one/ones

3 Complete the sentences with *one* or *ones*.

1 I don't usually like parties, but that was a good ___one___ .
2 These birthday cards are really expensive. Have you got any cheaper _____ ?
3 Which do you like best, the orange skirt or the red _____ ?
4 She wants some new trainers for her birthday. She doesn't like her old _____ .

Total: 3

Indefinite pronouns

4 Choose the correct options.

1 **Everything / Everyone** was having a good time at the party.
2 There's **nowhere / nothing** to do here. I'm bored.
3 There's **someone / something** in my eye. It really hurts!
4 **Everywhere / Everyone** I look, I can see books and paper.
5 I've got **nothing / something** to tell you, I'm getting married!
6 We always do **anything / something** on my birthday, we never stay at home.
7 Did you get Mum **anything / anyone** for Mother's Day?

Total: 6

too + adjective

5 Complete the sentences with the adjectives below and *too*.

expensive tired cold dangerous young ~~late~~ slow

1 Go to sleep. It's ___too late___ to play computer games.
2 I think it's _____ to go out without your coat. It's snowing outside!
3 You're _____ to play another game of tennis. Go and lie down!
4 I was _____ to catch the ball and it hit me in the face!
5 I'd like to try surfing but my mum says it's _____ .
6 My brother wants to buy this mobile phone but it's _____ .
7 My mum says I'm _____ to leave school so I have to study for another year.

Total: 6

(not) adjective + enough

6 Write *enough* in the correct place in the sentences.

1 One plastic bag wasn't big ∧ for all the shopping so we bought another one.   *enough*
2 Are you old to learn to drive in your country?
3 He's not strong to carry that.
4 My English isn't good to pass the exam.
5 It's not quiet to study in the library.
6 Can you run fast to win the race?

Total: 5

Language builder

7 **Complete the text with the correct options.**

Jan: We ¹_____ to WaveWorld next weekend. Do you want to come with us?

Pete: Yes, please! I ²_____ there.

Jan: It's a lot of fun! We ³_____ there last year. There are ⁴_____ really good water slides and ⁵_____ big wave pool. I think it's ⁶_____ than Watercity.

Pete: It sounds good! I ⁷_____ to go with you. I think it ⁸_____ be sunny on Saturday?

Jan: Yes, I hope so. And you won't be bored. There's always ⁹_____ to do because they've got lots of different rides.

Pete: I see. Which ride is ¹⁰_____ ?

Jan: I think the Bungee Jump is the best. I'll try that next time!

1 ⓐ are going   **b** go   **c** will go
2 a didn't go   **b** have never been
   c wasn't going
3 a have gone   **b** were going   **c** went
4 a much   **b** some   **c** a lot
5 a a   **b** some   **c** many
6 a best   **b** better   **c** good
7 a like   **b** don't like   **c** 'd like
8 a must   **b** can   **c** might
9 a somebody   **b** something   **c** nothing
10 a the exciting   **b** the most exciting
   c the more exciting

Total: 9

Vocabulary builder

8 **Circle the correct options.**

1 Most people _____ money when they want to buy a house or a car.
   ⓐ borrow   **b** buy   **c** earn

2 I'm _____ about going to the concert on Saturday.
   a sad   **b** angry   **c** excited

3 Nina wants to _____ to study Art and Design.
   a get a job   **b** leave school   **c** go to university

4 The road is icy. Don't _____ .
   a slip   **b** hurt   **c** break

5 This knife is really sharp. Don't _____ your finger.
   a cut   **b** bang   **c** burn

6 Tony banged his arm on the door and hurt his _____ .
   a ankle   **b** knee   **c** elbow

7 You can buy cereal in a cardboard _____ .
   a box   **b** tin   **c** jar

8 _____ your coat because it's cold.
   a Take off   **b** Get up   **c** Put on

9 We usually buy water in a plastic _____ .
   a jar   **b** bottle   **c** box

10 Some people dream _____ having a lot of money.
   a with   **b** about   **c** on

11 Your _____ is between your head and your arm.
   a chest   **b** shoulder   **c** back

12 Haley is _____ because her sister lost her favourite T-shirt.
   a tired   **b** bored   **c** angry

Total: 11

Speaking

9 **Put the sentences in the correct order to make a conversation.**

___ **A:** It's too cold and I'd rather go somewhere more interesting.
___ **A:** That's a great idea!
_1_ **A:** What shall we do on Saturday?
___ **B:** Let's go to the park. We can take our bikes.
___ **B:** Why don't we meet at ten outside the front entrance?
___ **B:** OK. How about going to the aquarium?

Total: 5

Total: 62

Indefinite pronouns

Remember that:

• we use singular verbs with indefinite pronouns.
  ✓ **Everyone** in my family **speaks** English.
  ✗ ~~Everyone in my family speak English.~~
• **nothing**, **nowhere**, and **no one** are negative. You do not need to make the sentence negative.
  ✓ **There is nothing** to do here at the weekend.
  ✗ ~~There isn't nothing to do here at the weekend.~~

1 Correct the sentences.
                  anything
  1 I don't have ~~nothing~~ ⟍to do on Friday night.
  2 There isn't nowhere to go in this town.
  3 He explained but I didn't understand nothing.
  4 I hope everything are OK.
  5 You don't have to invite nobody to come with you.

too + adjective and (*not*) + adjective + *enough*

Remember that:

• we use **too** + adjective to describe something. We never use *too much* + adjective.
  ✓ I am too tired to go out tonight.
  ✗ ~~I am too much tired to go out tonight.~~
• we use **not** and **too** <u>before</u> the adjective and **enough** <u>after</u> the adjective.
  ✓ He's **not old enough** to drive.
  ✗ ~~He's not enough old to drive.~~
• Be careful not to confuse **too** and **to**.
  ✓ I am **too tired to** go out tonight.
  ✗ ~~I am to tired to go out tonight.~~

2 Are the sentences correct? Correct the incorrect sentences.
  1 The weather wasn't enough good to have a picnic.
    The weather wasn't good enough to have a picnic.
  2 It's too much hot to study. Please open the window.
    _____
  3 Travelling by train is too much expensive and I'm not enough old to drive.
    _____
  4 The soup wasn't hot enough and the pizza was too cold.
    _____
  5 I'm tired too much to go out tonight.
    _____

Adjectives of feeling

Remember that:

• we use adjectives ending in **-ed** to say how a person feels.
  ✓ I play games on my phone when I'm **bored**.
  ✗ ~~I play games on my phone when I'm boring.~~
• we use adjectives ending in **-ing** to describe the things that cause the feelings.
  ✓ It was an **exciting** film.   ✗ ~~It was an excited film.~~

3 Choose the correct options.
  1 I was really (surprised) / surprising by his answer.
  2 They're very **interesting / interested** in the history of the city.
  3 This TV programme is **bored / boring**.
  4 I'm very **excited / exciting** about the wedding.
  5 I'm not going out. I'm too **tired / tiring**.

Spell it right! Difficult words

These words from the Student's Book are in the top 12 words that A2 students spell incorrectly most often. Remember to spell them correctly.

because	beautiful	tomorrow
comfortable	mobile	interesting
competition	address	birthday
hello		

4 <u>Underline</u> and correct the mistake in each sentence.
  1 My brother is unhealthy <u>becouse</u> he doesn't do sport.   *because*
  2 We stayed at a hotel in a beatiful forest in Wales.   _____
  3 We're going to watch a film in class tomorow.   _____
  4 The ice bed was more confortable than their bed at home.   _____
  5 I'm saving for a new mobil phone.   _____
  6 Elsa saw some intresting things at the museum yesterday.   _____
  7 Alice, you're the winner of our photography competion.   _____
  8 Please write your adress on this piece of paper.   _____
  9 I'm going to bake a cake for my brother's brithday.   _____
  10 They never smile or say hellow.   _____

Speaking extra

Shopping

1 ★ **Put the words in order to make questions and answers from the Real talk video in the Student's Book.**

1 do / money / How / you / your / spend / ?

_____

2 my / spend / food / I / money / usually / on

_____

3 love / friends / shopping / going / with / my / I

_____

4 friends / my / to / go / money / with / I / out / use

_____

5 spend / a / tickets / lot / of / on / I / concert / money

_____

2 ★★ 🔊 **09** **Listen and choose the correct answer.**

Conversation 1:

1 The girl wants to buy **a sweater** / **trainers**.

Conversation 2:

2 The boy wants to buy a **medium** / **large** T-shirt.

3 He prefers the **red** / **black** one.

Conversation 3:

4 The girl wants to buy **jeans** / **a shirt**.

5 She doesn't like the **size** / **colour**.

3 ★ **Read the conversation. Which game does Oliver buy?**

Oliver:	Excuse me, I'd ¹_____ to buy the new *MegaZoo 5* video game.
Shop assistant:	Sure, it's over there.
Oliver:	How ²_____ is it?
Shop assistant:	It's £26.99.
Oliver:	And how much is the *Doghouse* game?
Shop assistant:	It's £45.99.
Oliver:	OK, I think I'd ³_____ *MegaZoo 5*, then. Can I ⁴_____ the game first?
Shop assistant:	Yes, it's in this machine here.
Oliver:	Thanks.
Shop assistant:	⁵_____ is it?
Oliver:	It's great! I'll ⁶_____ it.

4 ★★ 🔊 **10** **Complete the conversation in Exercise 3 with the words in the box. Then listen and check.**

prefer	play	take	much	like	How

Focus on pronunciation

5 ★ 🔊 **11** **How do you say these prices? Listen and repeat.**

1 £1.99 **3** £180 **5** £10.50

2 £15 **4** £56.99

6 ★ 🔊 **12** **Listen to the conversation. What colour boots does Emily buy?**

Emily:	Excuse me, ¹_____ to a buy some boots.
Shop assistant:	Sure. What about these, or those ones over there?
Emily:	I think ²_____ them in black.
Shop assistant:	OK, over here. Do you like these?
Emily:	Yes, they're quite cool. ³_____ are they?
Shop assistant:	They're £65.99.
Emily:	⁴_____ them on?
Shop assistant:	Of course. ⁵_____ are you?
Emily:	I'm usually a size 7.
Shop assistant:	Here you are. How are they?
Emily:	I like them but have you got anything cheaper?
Shop assistant:	What about these? They're almost the same but they're £45.75 and they're brown.
Emily:	Yes, they're great! I'll ⁶_____ them.

7 ★★★ 🔊 **12** **Listen again and complete the conversation.**

8 ★★ 🔊 **12** **Listen again and check your answers. Then listen and repeat the conversation.**

Speaking extra

Speculating

1 ⭐ **Join the parts of the sentences from the Real talk video in the Student's Book.**

1　He can run faster
2　She's 20
3　She also helps
4　His family was very poor
5　He saved his little sister

a　a lot of children's charities.
b　and she's an amazing dancer.
c　but he worked hard and went to college.
d　from a burning house.
e　than anyone on the planet.

2 ⭐⭐ 🔊 **13 Listen and choose the correct answer.**

Conversation 1:
1　The boy and girl see **someone famous / a famous photographer**.

Conversation 2:
2　The boy and girl are at a **museum / bookshop**.
3　They **agree / don't agree** on what the picture is.

Conversation 3:
4　They are in a **History / Art** class.

3 ⭐ **Read the conversation. Match the jobs with the people in the photos.**

> dancer ___ 　 scientist ___
> musician ___ 　 firefighter ___

Boy: So what do we have to do?
Girl: You never listen, do you? We have to look at these photos and decide what jobs they do.
Boy: Just by looking at the photos.
Girl: Yes. So what do you ¹_____ he is?
Boy: Well, he ²_____ very strong … and brave, I think. So a firefighter, something like that.

Girl: Yeah, I agree. This guy looks very serious but he's got a friendly face. He ³_____ be an artist.
Boy: Yes, but look at the way he's standing. I ⁴_____ he's a dancer.
Girl: Oh yeah. You're right. What about this woman?
Boy: I'm not ⁵_____ .
Girl: Well, she's wearing a white coat so could be either a scientist or a nurse.
Boy: That's ⁶_____ .
Girl: She ⁷_____ works in a laboratory so she's a scientist.
Boy: Right. What about this woman?
Girl: I reckon she's a musician.
Boy: OK, write it down. Come on, let's check our answers.

4 ⭐⭐ 🔊 **14 Complete the conversation in Exercise 3 with the words in the box. Then listen and check.**

> reckon 　 possible 　 looks 　 think
> definitely 　 could 　 sure

Focus on pronunciation

5 ⭐ 🔊 **15 Listen to the sentences. Do they go up or down? Listen and repeat.**

1　I'm not sure.
2　That's possible.
3　She could be a vet.
4　I reckon she's an artist.

6 ⭐ 🔊 **16 Listen to the conversation. Whose phone is it?**

Mark: Look! A mobile phone.
Olivia: Oh yeah, whose ¹_____ ?
Mark: I'm ²_____ . It's ³_____ someone from our class because it's in our classroom.
Olivia: ⁴_____ very new. Do you think it's the teacher's phone?
Mark: ⁵_____ . ⁶_____ it's a student's phone. Look at the photo here.
Olivia: Oh yeah. She's definitely not in our class.
Mark: ⁷_____ someone's sister or cousin.
Olivia: You're right. Hold on. ⁸_____ it's Vanessa's – I've seen Vanessa with that dress on so that could be her sister.
Mark: Right, let's go and find her.

7 ⭐⭐⭐ 🔊 **16 Listen again and complete the conversation.**

Speaking extra

Telling someone your news

1 ★ **Complete the sentences from the Real talk video in the Student's Book with the words in the box.**

> the lock   the winning goal   a new shirt   my cat

1 A couple of weeks ago _____ Jasper escaped.
2 The bike was still there but _____ wasn't.
3 I scored _____ in the last five minutes of the game.
4 Last weekend I wore _____ to my friend's birthday party and she was wearing the same one.

2 ★★ 🔊 **17 Listen and write the answers.**

Conversation 1:
1 What month is it?
_____

Conversation 2:
2 What was the boy doing?
_____

3 What kind of animal flew into the window?
_____

Conversation 3:
4 What are they talking about?
_____

3 ★ **Read the conversation. What did Andy find in the park?**

Andy:	Did you hear about this morning?
Louise:	No, what?
Andy:	Something ¹_____ happened while we were walking to school. We heard a baby crying in the park. But we couldn't see anyone.
Louise:	So ²_____ did you do?
Andy:	We started looking for it – the sound got louder and louder. It was coming from a park bench.
Louise:	So did you find it?
Andy:	No, because it wasn't a baby! It was a mobile phone! I answered it and a man started shouting at me!
Louise:	What did you ³_____ ?
Andy:	At first, I didn't know what to say and then, I said, 'I'm sorry. You've got the wrong number.'
Louise:	What happened ⁴_____ ?
Andy:	Another man ran up to us and said it was his phone, so we gave it to him. He said something about his boss being really angry. And then he ran off again.
Louise:	How ⁵_____ !

4 ★★ 🔊 **18 Complete the conversation in Exercise 3 with the words in the box. Then listen and check your answers.**

> next   what   unusual   do   weird

Focus on pronunciation

5 ★ 🔊 **19 Listen to the words and phrases. Do they go up or down? Listen and repeat.**

1 Really?   4 I know!
2 What?   5 Cool!
3 How weird!

6 ★ 🔊 **20 Listen to the conversation. Who were the photographers waiting for?**

Ben:	¹_____ happened yesterday.
Peter:	What?
Ben:	I was walking out of the school and I saw lots of photographers waiting at the door.
Peter:	²_____ .
Ben:	I know. I didn't understand what they were doing there.
Peter:	So ³_____ ?
Ben:	Well, I waited on the other side of the street. Then Mrs Carter, our History teacher, came out. And all the photographers started taking photos of her.
Peter:	Really? Your History teacher? ⁴_____ ?
Ben:	Well, they started asking her questions about money.
Peter:	Money? And ⁵_____ ?
Ben:	She said she was really happy.

7 ★★★ 🔊 **20 Listen again and complete the conversation.**

8 ★★ 🔊 **20 Listen again and check your answers. Then listen and repeat the conversation.**

9 ★ 🔊 **21 Listen to the end of the conversation. What happened?**

Speaking extra

Asking for and offering help

1 ★ **Complete the sentences from the Real talk video in the Student's Book with the words in the box.**

> garden   quieter   expensive   space   rooms   light

1   They're usually bigger so there's more
    _____ .
2   I think houses because they can be _____ .
3   Flats are small and they sometimes don't get
    much _____ .
4   It has a lot of _____ and it's really
    comfortable.
5   There isn't usually a _____ with a flat.
6   Houses near the centre of big cities are really
    _____ .

2 ★★ 🔊 22 **Listen and answer the questions.**
Conversation 1:
1   How does the boy help the woman?
    _____

Conversation 2:
2   What did Sarah leave at school?
    _____

3   Where will Helen go later?
    _____

Conversation 3:
4   What does the boy have to do?
    _____

5   What does the girl want?
    _____

3 ★ **Read the conversation. What do Connor and Jonas put in the wardrobe?**

Connor:	My mum says I should tidy my room before I go out.
Jonas:	Well, she's right. I'll ¹_____ you a hand.
Connor:	OK, let's see. The books shouldn't be on the floor. I should put them all up on that shelf.
Jonas:	Here, ²_____ do that. Oh look, *The Lord of the Rings*. Did you like it?
Connor:	Yes, it's really good. Can you ³_____ me a favour?
Jonas:	Yes, of ⁴_____ .
Connor:	Can you give me a ⁵_____ and put this blanket in the wardrobe?
Jonas:	⁶_____ I put this pillow in there as well?
Connor:	Yes, please!

4 ★★ 🔊 23 **Complete the conversation in Exercise 3 with the words in the box. Then listen and check.**

> do   I'll   give   Shall   course   hand

Focus on pronunciation

5 ★ 🔊 24 **Listen to the questions. Do they go up or down? Listen and repeat.**
1   Can you give me a hand?
2   Can you put this on the shelf?
3   Can you do me a favour?
4   Can you help me with this?

6 ★ 🔊 25 **Listen to the conversation. What do Nick and Lisa put in the freezer?**

Nick:	Come on, the computer's ready. Let's play.
Lisa:	Hang on. I can't. My dad did the shopping and he wants me to put it all away.
Nick:	OK, I'll give you ¹_____ .
Lisa:	Great. That way we'll finish sooner.
Nick:	²_____ put the milk and cheese in the fridge?
Lisa:	Yes, please!
Nick:	Anything else?
Lisa:	We should put the ice cream and the pizzas in the freezer.
Nick:	³_____ !
Lisa:	And I need to wash all this fruit. ⁴_____ me a hand?
Nick:	Sure: Put it all in the sink and ⁵_____ .
Lisa:	Oh and another thing. Can you do me ⁶_____ ?
Nick:	Sure.
Lisa:	Can you start making lunch? I'm hungry!
Nick:	Ha ha ha! Come on. Mario is waiting!

7 ★★★ 🔊 25 **Listen again and complete the conversation.**

8 ★★ 🔊 25 **Listen again and check your answers. Then listen and repeat the conversation.**

Speaking extra

Asking for and giving instructions

1 ★ **Match the sentence halves from the Real talk video in the Student's Book.**

1 I don't have a phone
2 It's more important to my mum
3 It's not really important to me.
4 I use it for the games and the apps
5 My mum tells me to take it with me

a so she can call me any time she wants.
b and I watch my favourite TV programmes on it.
c whenever I go out.
d so it's not important to me at all.
e I usually leave it at home.

2 ★★ 🔊 26 **Listen and answer the questions.**

Conversation 1:

1 What does the girl want to see?

_____

Conversation 2:

2 What does the girl need to do to get on to the website?

_____

3 How does she start playing?

_____

Conversation 3:

4 What are they trying to do?

_____

3 ★ **Read the conversation. What does Daniel teach his granddad to do on the tablet?**

Granddad:	That looks exciting. What is it?
Daniel:	It's a tablet. It's a kind of computer.
Grandad:	Oh, I see. How does it ¹_____ ?
Daniel:	It's easy. ²_____ , you need to press the button on the top.
Granddad:	This one?
Daniel:	Yes, ³_____ it. Now, if you swipe your finger across the touchscreen, it'll turn on the apps.
Granddad:	Apps?
Daniel:	Yes, look, you just ⁴_____ to touch one with your finger.
Granddad:	Oh but, what is it?
Daniel:	It's a game. It's called *Dogs in Space*.
Granddad:	Oh no! How do I turn the music down?
Daniel:	Find the button on the side.
Granddad:	OK, ⁵_____ it is.
Daniel:	Then press it a few times.
Granddad:	So ⁶_____ do I stop it?
Daniel:	Press the button at the top again.
Granddad:	Oh, what's that noise?
Daniel:	I just got an email.

4 ★★ 🔊 27 **Complete the conversation in Exercise 3 with the words in the box. Then listen and check your answers.**

> have here work how that's First

Focus on pronunciation

5 ★ 🔊 28 **Listen to the instructions. Do they go up or down? Which instruction goes down? Listen and repeat.**

1 First, click on this icon.
2 Now, look for the name of the person.
3 Now, you have to scroll down the list.
4 Then, you click on the name.
5 And just click on the green button.

6 ★ 🔊 29 **Listen to the conversation. Why does Hugh's dad put his hand on the screen?**

Dad:	I want to get on this social network. How ¹_____ ?
Hugh:	Let's see. First, you ²_____ create a profile.
Dad:	Err … a profile. OK, ³_____ do that?
Hugh:	Click here and put in your name and all your information.
Dad:	All this?
Hugh:	No. You only have to put in the things with the red stars: your name, your email and a password. Now, scroll down and just click on 'Create Profile'.
Dad:	Oh, I see. ⁴_____ ?
Hugh:	Yes! That's it. If you click here, you'll get an email.
Dad:	OK, here it is. It says 'confirm your profile'. How do I confirm my profile?
Hugh:	Just click on the link in the email.
Dad:	I see! Thanks!
Hugh:	And ⁵_____ put your hand on the screen and say 'Hello', your friends will say 'Hello' too.
Dad:	OK … 'Hello?'
Hugh:	Haha! Very good, Dad, but you don't really have to do that!
Dad:	Hey!

7 ★★★ 🔊 29 **Listen again and complete the conversation.**

8 ★★ 🔊 29 **Listen again and check your answers. Then listen and repeat the conversation.**

Speaking extra

Agreeing and disagreeing

1 ★ **Put the words in order to make sentences from the Real talk video in the Student's Book.**

1 know / yet / don't / I / going / what / I'm / to do

_____

2 go / to / and / Chinese / I'm / going / to / university / study

_____

3 player / going / be / a / I'm / football / to / professional

_____

4 around / I'm / motorcycle / going / world / to / buy / a / ride / and / the

_____

2 ★★ 🔊 **30 Listen and answer the questions.**

Conversation 1:

1 What does the girl think about education?

_____

Conversation 2:

2 Does the boy agree with the girl?

_____

3 Which word does he use to describe homework?

_____

Conversation 3:

4 What is the topic of their discussion?

_____

3 ★ **Read the conversation. How many statements do Alex and Julie discuss?**

Alex: OK, I want you to give me your opinion about some different topics.

Julie: Sure. What topics?

Alex: Well, I have some statements about young people's lives and I need you to tell me if you agree or disagree with them.

Julie: OK. Go on then.

Alex: Let's see, first statement: Young people should get married later, for example, after university or when they have a job. Do you ¹_____ ?

Julie: I'm not ²_____ I do agree. I think young people should get married when they want or when they're old enough to get married in their country.

Alex: OK, next one: Too many young people go to university. What's your ³_____ ?

Julie: No, I ⁴_____ . I think young people should be able to continue their studies when they leave school if they want to.

Alex: I agree ⁵_____ you. And here's the last statement: Going to university helps you get a better job.

Julie: Absolutely! Young people who go to university can get better jobs because they know more things.

Alex: Yes, I ⁶_____ you're right. But they should be able to get a job when they leave school if that's what they want to do.

4 ★★ 🔊 **31 Complete the conversation in Exercise 3 with the words in the box. Then listen and check.**

with   agree   disagree   suppose   sure   opinion

Focus on pronunciation

5 ★ 🔊 **32 Listen. Do the words and phrases go up or down? Listen and repeat.**

1 Absolutely.

2 I agree with you.

3 I suppose you're right.

4 Maybe, but I also think it's difficult.

5 I disagree.

6 ★ 🔊 **33 Listen to the conversation. Where is Jessica going?**

Reporter: Excuse me! Can you give us five minutes? We'd like to know your opinion on some different topics.

Jessica: OK. What are the topics?

Reporter: Well, here's the first one: Life is more difficult now than it was for your parents. Do ¹_____ ?

Jessica: No, ²_____ . I think life is easier now, especially because of technology.

Reporter: OK. ³_____ think life will be easier in the future than it is now?

Jessica: Maybe, but I ⁴_____ we'll have a lot of problems … especially with the environment.

Reporter: Thanks. Next one: We'll probably live on other planets in the future. What's ⁵_____ ?

Jessica: ⁶_____ ! There are too many of us here on Earth!

Reporter: ⁷_____ you're right. But where would we go?

Jessica: I don't know but right now, I'm going home.

Reporter: Oh, yes, thanks for your time. Bye!

7 ★★★ 🔊 **33 Listen again and complete the conversation.**

Speaking extra

Reacting to news

1 ★ **Match the sentence halves from the Real talk video in the Student's Book.**

1 I fell out of a tree and
2 I've broken my leg twice
3 I cut my hand
4 I've sprained my wrists
5 I was playing in the kitchen

a a lot of times playing volleyball.
b on a broken glass last week and it still hurts.
c but I can still run faster than all my friends.
d and I burned my hand on the oven.
e sprained my ankle when I was five.

2 ★★ 🔊 **34 Listen and answer the questions.**

Conversation 1:

1 What happened to David last week?

_____

Conversation 2:

2 What's wrong with Lisa?

_____

Conversation 3:

3 Where did Charlie go on holiday?

_____

4 What part of her body did Anne burn?

_____

3 ★ **Read the conversation. Did something good happen to Liam or Abby?**

Abby:	Hi, Liam, how's it ¹_____ ?
Liam:	Fine thanks, Abby. How about you?
Abby:	Yeah, not bad. I've got a place at university. I'm going to study Physics.
Liam:	Well done! That's ²_____ .
Abby:	Thanks. I'm really excited. What have you been ³_____ to?
Liam:	Well, I cut my knee while I was playing football at school. Look!
Abby:	Oh no! How did you do that?
Liam:	I don't know really – I fell over and another boy kicked me with his boot. When I got home, I couldn't move my leg.
Abby:	What a ⁴_____ ! When did it happen?
Liam:	Last Monday. It's getting better now but I can't play football for a few weeks.
Abby:	I'm sorry to ⁵_____ that.
Liam:	So, tell me about your new university …

4 ★★ 🔊 **35 Complete the conversation in Exercise 3 with the words in the box. Then listen and check your answers.**

> up   shame   fantastic   hear   going

Focus on pronunciation

5 ★ 🔊 **36 Listen. Do the phrases go up or down? Listen and repeat.**

1 Oh no!
2 What a shame!
3 I'm sorry to hear that!
4 How amazing!
5 That's fantastic!

6 ★ 🔊 **37 Listen to the conversation. Why can't Matthew go to London?**

Lucy:	Hi, Matthew, ¹_____ ?
Matthew:	Oh, hi, Lucy, fine thanks. How about you?
Lucy:	Not bad, yeah. I've just been in that shop over there. I was trying on dresses for a wedding.
Matthew:	²_____ ! Are you getting married?
Lucy:	No! It's my brother. He's getting married in June … in London.
Matthew:	In London? ³_____ !
Lucy:	So … em, Matthew, ⁴_____ ?
Matthew:	Not a lot really. Studying, you know. I didn't pass my Maths exam so I have to do it again in June.
Lucy:	⁵_____ ! In June?
Matthew:	Yeah, I'm going to take the exam on 5 June.
Lucy:	The 5th? ⁶_____ !
Matthew:	Why?
Lucy:	Well, that's the day my brother's getting married and … well, I wanted to invite you to come to London with me.
Matthew:	Me? Really? Oh … sorry. I have to do my Maths exam!
Lucy:	Well, ⁷_____ , Matthew.
Matthew:	Yes. Me too.

7 ★★★ 🔊 **37 Listen again and complete the conversation.**

8 ★★ 🔊 **37 Listen again and check your answers. Then listen and repeat the conversation.**

Speaking extra

Suggesting and responding

1 ★ **Complete the sentences from the Real talk video in the Student's Book with the verbs in the box.**

wore   celebrate   invite   took   go on   have

1 I always _____ a big party and _____ everyone in my class.
2 I prefer to _____ my birthday at home with my family.
3 I usually _____ a trip with my friends or family.
4 Everybody _____ pink and all the food was pink too.
5 I didn't celebrate it. I _____ an exam.

2 ★★ 🔊 38 **Listen and answer the questions.**

Conversation 1:
1 What are they going to do on Saturday?
_____

Conversation 2:
2 Why is tomorrow a special day?
_____

3 What are they going to do?
_____

Conversation 3:
4 What would the girl prefer to do?
_____

5 What do they decide to eat?
_____

3 ★ **Read the conversation. Where are Ella and Mary going? Why?**

Ella: What [1]_____ we do on Sunday?
Mary: Sunday? Why?
Ella: It's my birthday. Don't you remember?
Mary: Oh, yeah! [2]_____ have a party with everybody from our class.
Ella: OK, why not? Where?
Mary: What [3]_____ having it at your house?
Ella: My house isn't big enough. I think I'd [4]_____ go out.
Mary: OK, how about meeting everyone from school for a meal somewhere?
Ella: That's a nice [5]_____ ! Why [6]_____ we go to that new pizza restaurant in town?
Mary: Fantastic. I'm excited already!
Ella: OK, let's call the others.

4 ★★ 🔊 39 **Complete the conversation in Exercise 3 with the words in the box. Then listen and check.**

don't   Let's   rather   about   idea   shall

Focus on pronunciation

5 ★ 🔊 40 **Listen to the questions. Do they go up or down? Listen and repeat.**

1 How about having a party?
2 Let's watch a film.
3 Why don't we have a meal?
4 What about meeting some friends?
5 Where shall we go tomorrow?

6 ★ 🔊 41 **Listen to the conversation. What will Julie do at the party?**

Mike: You know it's Dad's birthday in two weeks? He's 55.
Julie: Oh, yeah! [1]_____ ?
Mike: Well, I was thinking … [2]_____ have a surprise party?
Julie: [3]_____! We can invite all the family and a few friends.
Mike: OK, but where shall we have it? Our house is too small.
Julie: [4]_____ calling Uncle Dave? He's got a big house and a big garden. It's big enough for about 20 people.
Mike: Yes, I'm sure he'll agree.
Julie: What about asking Mum and Auntie Jean to make some food?
Mike: OK, [5]_____ ? But we'll have to help them.
Julie: Help them? You know I can't cook. I think [6]_____ organise the music.
Mike: You can organise the music but you have to talk to Uncle Dave too.
Julie: Uncle Dave loves me! I'm sure he'll say yes.

7 ★★★ 🔊 41 **Listen again and complete the conversation.**

8 ★★ 🔊 41 **Listen again and check your answers. Then listen and repeat the conversation.**

Language focus extra

Subject pronouns and *be*

1 Complete the questions with *am, is* or *are*.
Then match the question with the answer.

1 When _____*is*_____ your birthday?   _*c*_
2 _____ your friends at home?   _____
3 How old _____ your aunt?   _____
4 What time _____ it?   _____
5 _____ you from Chile?   _____

a No, they aren't.
b It's 10 o'clock.
c It's on 2 June.
d No, I'm not.
e She's 48.

Possessive *'s*

2 Add *'s* or *'* to the correct place in the sentences.
1 Martin's pencil case is black and white.
2 My best friend bike is in the sports hall.
3 My parents names are Cristina and Robbie.
4 My cousin friends are in my class.
5 My three friends books are on the floor.

there is/are + *some* and *any*

3 Match the sentence halves.
1 There isn't   _*c*_
2 Are there   _____
3 There aren't   _____
4 There's   _____
5 Is there   _____

a any orange juice in that bag?
b some water in the canteen.
c any milk on the table.
d any computers in your school library?
e any dictionaries in our classroom.

Have got + *a/an*

4 Read about Rachel, Ben and Tom's things
and complete the table with answers about
you. Use the information to write Yes/No
questions with *have* and short answers.

	Rachel	Ben and Tom	You
a dog or a cat	✓	✗	_____
a laptop	✗	✓	_____

1 *Has Rachel got a dog or a cat?*   *Yes, she has.*
2 *Has Rachel got a laptop?*   _____
3 _____ ?   _____

4 _____ ?   _____
5 _____ ?   _____
6 _____ ?   _____

Present simple: affirmative and negative

5 Write sentences with the correct form of the
present simple.
1 I / not ride / my bike to school
   I don't ride my bike to school.
2 My friends / play / basketball in the school team
   _____
3 My teacher / go / swimming in the sea every day
   _____
4 We / not have / lunch at home
   _____
5 My dad / not work / near here
   _____

Present simple: questions

6 Put the words in order to make questions and
write the answers.
1 you / Where / do / live / ?
   Where do you live? I live near my school.
2 you and your friends / snowboarding / Do / go / ?
   _____
3 lunch / What time / you / have / do / ?
   _____
4 Does / mum / skiing / go / your / ?
   _____
5 dinner / dad / Does / TV / after / your / watch / ?
   _____

Adverbs of frequency

7 Circle the correct words.
1 I (often play) / play often volleyball in the
   summer.
2 My sister and I **do usually** / **usually do** our
   homework in our bedroom.
3 I **am sometimes** / **sometimes am** tired on
   Monday morning.
4 We **sometimes go** / **go sometimes** surfing.
5 It **is never** / **never is** hot in December.

Language focus extra

Present continuous: affirmative and negative

1 Complete the sentences with the present continuous form of the verb in brackets.

1 Lots of people __are shopping__ in the mall today. (shop)
2 I _____ for a new dress. (look)
3 My mum _____ a magazine in the cafe. (read)
4 She _____ coffee. (not drink)
5 My brother _____ a computer game. (play)
6 We _____ a lot of money. (not spend)

Present continuous: *Wh-* questions

2 Write questions using the present continuous.

1 What / you / buy
__What are you buying_____ ?
2 Where / they / go
_____ ?
3 Who / she / meet
_____ ?
4 What / Jenny / watch
_____ ?
5 Why / we / wait
_____ ?
6 What / Joe / wear
_____ ?

Present continuous: *Yes/No* questions

3 Read what Maria, Judy and Tim are doing and complete the table with answers about you. Use the information to write *Yes/No* questions and short answers in the present continuous.

	Maria	Judy and Tim	You
visit the mall	✗	✓	_____
study grammar	✓	✗	_____

1 __Is Maria visiting the mall__ ? __No__ , __she isn't__ .
2 _____ ? _____ , _____ .
3 _____ ? _____ , _____ .
4 _____ ? _____ , _____ .
5 _____ ? _____ , _____ .
6 _____ ? _____ , _____ .

Spelling: *-ing* form

4 Complete the chart with the *-ing* form of the verbs in the box.

~~do~~ get look make run write

Add *-ing*	Remove the *-e* and add *-ing*	Double consonant and add *-ing*
1 _doing_	3 _____	5 _____
2 _____	4 _____	6 _____

Present simple vs. continuous

5 Complete the sentences with the present simple or present continuous form of the verbs in the box.

buy not do ~~eat~~ not talk visit

1 We __are eating__ pizza right now.
2 I _____ my homework at the moment.
3 They often _____ the mall on Saturdays.
4 My mum _____ books in that shop.
5 Joe _____ on his mobile right now.

(don't) want to, would(n't) like to, would prefer to

6 (Circle) the correct options.

1 I don't (want)/ like to go to school today.
2 Jack likes playing football but he'd **want / prefer** to go swimming today.
3 Would you **want / like** to come with me?
4 I wouldn't **like / prefer** to do judo.
5 We've got Maths and English homework today. I'd **want / prefer** to do English first.

(not) enough + noun

7 Complete the sentences with *enough* and the words in the box.

money milk ~~paper~~ chairs time

1 There isn't __enough__ __paper__ for everyone.
2 I'd like to buy a skateboard but I haven't got _____ _____ .
3 Sit down, everybody. Oh sorry, we haven't got _____ _____ .
4 We can't go to the bookshop now. We haven't got _____ _____ . It's late.
5 Have you got _____ _____ for three glasses?

Language focus extra

was/were: affirmative and negative

1 Complete the sentences with the correct form of *was* or *were*.

At school, I¹ <u>wasn't</u> (not) very good at sport but I² _____ good at dancing. My friends ³ _____ all crazy about football. They ⁴ _____ (not) interested in dancing. I saw my first ballet when I⁵ _____ 12 years old. It⁶ _____ amazing!

Past simple: affirmative and negative

2 Write sentences in the past simple.

1 Tim / play / football / yesterday
   <u>Tim played football yesterday.</u>

2 Joanna / go skiing / last winter
   _____

3 Gina and Tony / grow up / in Canada
   _____

4 We / not want / to practise the piano / last weekend
   _____

5 I / not play / tennis / at school / when I was little
   _____

6 Nicky / not win / the singing competition / last week
   _____

Past simple: irregular verbs

3 Write the past simple of each verb.

1 have _____ *had*
2 make _____
3 become _____
4 write _____
5 get _____
6 see _____

Past simple: spelling

4 Complete the chart with the past simple form of each verb.

| like   stop   dance   study   try   ~~wait~~ |

Add *-ed*	Add *-d*
1 <u>waited</u>	2 _____
	3 _____

Remove the last letter and add *-ied*	Double the last consonant and add *-ed*
4 _____	6 _____
5 _____	

was/were: questions

5 Complete the questions with the past simple of *be* and write the short answers.

1 <u>Were</u> you in judo class yesterday?
   <u>Yes, I was</u> . ✓

2 _____ Jake good at sports at school?
   _____ . ✓

3 _____ they in the supermarket this morning? No, _____ . ✗

4 _____ he unfriendly at the party?
   _____ . ✗

5 _____ your cousin Julia in Paris last year?
   _____ . ✓

6 _____ the police officers at your school yesterday? _____ . ✓

Past simple: *Wh-* questions

6 Write a question for each answer. Use the past simple.

1 What <u>did you drink</u> ?
   I drank some lemonade.

2 Where _____ ?
   He went to a concert.

3 When _____ ?
   They started school at 9 am.

4 Who _____ ?
   She met her sister.

5 What _____ ?
   We ate some sandwiches.

6 Why _____ ?
   We stayed at home because it was raining.

Past simple: *Yes/No* questions

7 Read what Helen, Sam and Abby did last weekend and complete the table with answers about you. Use the information to write *Yes/No* questions and short answers in the past simple.

	Helen	Sam and Abby	You
eat pizza	✗	✓	_____
go shopping	✓	✗	_____

1 <u>Did Helen eat pizza</u> ? <u>No</u> , <u>she didn't</u> .
2 _____ ? _____ , _____ .
3 _____ ? _____ , _____ .
4 _____ ? _____ , _____ .
5 _____ ? _____ , _____ .
6 _____ ? _____ , _____ .

Language focus extra

Past continuous: affirmative

1 **Complete the sentences with the past continuous forms of the verbs in the box.**

> cook   chase   drink   ~~read~~   steal   talk   buy   watch

At 3 pm yesterday afternoon …
1 …Peter _was reading_ a book.
2 …Julie _____ on the phone.
3 …Jason and Angie _____ dinner.
4 …we _____ TV.
5 …I _____ a cup of tea.
6 … the burglars _____ the money.
7 … my parents _____ a new car.
8 … the dog _____ the cat around the house.

Past continuous: negative

2 **Complete the sentences with the negative form of the past continuous. Use contractions.**

1 Peter ___wasn't playing___ football. (play)
2 Julie _____ emails. (write)
3 Jason and Angie _____ in the garden. (sit)
4 We _____ our bikes. (ride)
5 I _____ a sandwich. (eat)
6 The burglars _____ any noise. (make)
7 My parents _____ to the shop. (walk)
8 The dog _____ in the park. (run)

Past continuous: *Wh-* questions

3 **Write *Wh-* questions with the past continuous.**

1 What ___were you doing___ ? (you / do)
2 Where _____ ? (they / go)
3 Who _____ ? (she / talk to)
4 Why _____ ? (he / leave)
5 Where _____ ? (Jacky / sit)
6 What _____ ? (your friends / watch)
7 Why _____ ? (they / go)
8 Who _____ ? (she / meet)

Past continuous: *Yes/No* questions

4 **Read what Jessica, Luke and Nina were doing at 5 pm yesterday and complete the table with answers about you. Then use the information to write *Yes/No* questions and short answers with the past continuous.**

	Jessica	Luke and Nina	You
watch TV	✗	✓	_____
do homework	✓	✗	_____

1 _Was Jessica watching TV_ ? _No_ , _she wasn't_ .
2 _____ ? _____ , _____ .
3 _____ ? _____ , _____ .
4 _____ ? _____ , _____ .
5 _____ ? _____ , _____ .
6 _____ ? _____ , _____ .

Past simple vs. continuous

5 **Complete the sentences with the past simple or the past continuous.**

1 I _was reading_ (read) in bed when I _____ (hear) a loud noise in the street.
2 No one _____ (watch) when the burglars _____ (break) into the bank.
3 The money _____ (disappear) while the guards _____ (have) lunch.
4 While we _____ (watch) TV, the alarm _____ (go) off.
5 When we _____ (look) out of the window, police officers _____ (enter) the bank.
6 The burglars _____ (count) their money when the police _____ (catch) them.

could(n't)

6 **Complete the sentences with *could/couldn't* and the words in brackets.**

1 I _could speak_ French when I was five. (speak)
2 She _____ because she was afraid of water. (not swim)
3 Sam _____ the top shelf because he was too short. (not reach)
4 _____ the piano when he was small? (Tony, play)
5 We _____ because he spoke very quietly. (not hear)
6 _____ a bike when you were a child? (you, ride)

Language focus extra

Comparatives

1 Complete the table with the comparative forms of the words in the box.

> comfortable expensive nice
> interesting safe tall

Add -r or -er	more + adjective
_____	more comfortable
_____	_____
_____	_____

2 Complete the sentences with the comparative form of the words in brackets.

1 My house is _smaller than_ your house. (small)
2 Jack's room is _____ Katrina's room. (tidy)
3 Laura's homework is _____ Abby's homework. (good)
4 This new hotel is _____ the old hotel. (comfortable)
5 The sofa is _____ the armchair. (expensive)

Superlatives

3 Write superlative sentences with the words below.

1 The New South China Mall / large / shopping centre / world
The New South China Mall is the largest shopping centre in the world.

2 Vostok in Antarctica / cold / place on Earth
_____

3 My bedroom / good / room in the house
_____

4 This is / comfortable / chair
_____

5 I'm not / bad / student / in our class
_____

Comparatives and superlatives

4 Circle the correct form.

1 **A:** I think New York is **more exciting / the most exciting** city in the world!
   B: I don't agree. I think that London is **more exciting / the most exciting** than New York.
2 **A:** Buses are **safer / the safest** than trains.
   B: I don't agree. I think that trains are **safer / the safest** form of transport.
3 **A:** I think that Tokyo is **more expensive / the most expensive** city in the world.
   B: I read that Singapore is **more expensive / the most expensive** than Tokyo.

must/mustn't

5 Complete the sentences with *must* or *mustn't* and the verb in brackets.

1 You _mustn't talk_ during the lesson. (talk)
2 You _____ your homework on time. (do)
3 You _____ sandwiches in the classroom. (eat)
4 You _____ your friend's homework. (copy)
5 You _____ on the chairs. (stand)
6 You _____ carefully to the teacher. (listen)

should/shouldn't

6 Complete the sentences with *should* or *shouldn't* and the verbs in the box.

> take go meet phone stay wear

1 It's cold today. You _should wear_ a warm coat.
2 The train leaves at 10 am. We _____ at 9.45.
3 It's raining. You _____ your umbrella.
4 It's late. You _____ to bed now.
5 I've got an exam tomorrow. I _____ up late.
6 You've got a toothache. You _____ the dentist.

should/shouldn't: questions

7 Put the words in the correct order to make questions. Then complete the answers.

1 we / Should / get up / tomorrow / early
   A: _Should we get up early tomorrow_ ?
   B: Yes, _we should_ .
2 wear / I / to the party / should / What
   A: _____ ?
   B: You _____ your blue dress.
3 use / my calculator / in the exam / Should / I
   A: _____ ?
   B: No, _____
4 we / When / meet / should
   A: _____ ?
   B: We _____ at 9 am.
5 Should / book / I / a hotel
   A: _____ ?
   B: Yes, _____
6 What / do / should / this afternoon / I
   A: _____ ?
   B: You _____ your homework.

Language focus extra

will/won't

1 **Complete the text with _will_ and the words in the box.**

| be   do   ~~go~~   have   study   work |

My plans for the future: first, I ¹___*will go*___
to university and I ²_____ Engineering.
I think that Engineering ³_____ very
important because we ⁴_____ so many new
developments in science and technology. Then I
⁵_____ research at a university in Australia.
After that, I ⁶_____ in a company to make
new inventions.

2 **Circle the correct words.**
Children ¹will / **won't** go to school because they
²**will** / won't study at home. We ³**will** / won't have
electric cars because there ⁴will / **won't** be enough
petrol. People ⁵will / **won't** work in factories because
robots ⁶**will** / won't do all the work.

will/won't questions

3 **Write questions with _will_. Then write short
answers.**

1 robots / clean our homes
_Will robots clean our homes? Yes, they will._____ ✓

2 all countries / speak one language
_____ ✗

3 aeroplanes / be faster
_____ ✓

4 the climate / be warmer
_____ ✗

5 people / live longer
_____ ✓

6 the world / be more peaceful
_____ ✓

may/might

4 **Put the words in order to make sentences.**

1 smartphone / buy / tomorrow / might / a / new / I
_I might buy a new smartphone tomorrow.____

2 may / new / in / room / desk / a / put / We / your
_____

3 might / the / before / shopping / not / lunch /
mum / My / do
_____

4 tired / lie / may / I / because / I'm / down
_____

5 Jenny / may / you / think / Do / unhappy / be / ?
_____

will/won't, may/might

5 **Complete the sentences with the correct form
of _may_, _might_, _will_ or _won't_. Sometimes more
than one answer is possible.**

1 I think I ___*might*___ do my homework now.
I don't know.

2 I'm not sure but I think it _____ rain
tomorrow.

3 I'm sure the teacher _____ give us
homework tomorrow.

4 We _____ have our Maths class later
because our teacher is not here.

5 The chocolate _____ be in the fridge. Have
a look!

6 I know that my tablet _____ be here
when I come back because it's very safe.

First conditional

6 **Match the sentence halves.**

1 If you turn on the computer, *c*
2 If I don't leave now,
3 If you don't have a computer,
4 We will learn how to make a website,
5 You will get a better job
6 I won't pass the exam

a I will miss the train.
b if I don't study tonight.
c I'll show you my new website.
d if you learn about technology.
e you won't be able to check your email.
f if we go on this course.

First conditional: questions

7 **Make questions in the first conditional with
the words below.**

1 What / you / do / your computer / breaks
_What will you do if your computer breaks_____ ?

2 you / go home / class / finish early
_____ ?

3 How / Stacy / check her email / she / not have a
computer
_____ ?

4 they / call / us / they / miss the train
_____ ?

5 What / Danny / do / not get the job
_____ ?

6 Jessica / buy a car / pass / her driving test
_____ ?

Language focus extra

be going to

1 Complete the sentences with the correct form of *be going to* and the words in the box.

> buy   get   not go   ~~study~~   take   work

1 I _am going to study_ History at university.
2 Rita _____ in her dad's shop this summer.
3 My brother _____ a year out after university.
4 My parents _____ a new house next year.
5 Sam and Linda _____ married next year.
6 We _____ to summer camp this year.

be going to: questions

2 Write questions and short answers with *be going to*.
1 What _are you going to do_ this summer? (you, do)
2 Where _____ next year? (Tina, work)
3 When _____ ? (your parents, arrive)
4 _____ this summer ? (they, visit Canada)
  No, they _____ .
5 _____ next year? (I, learn to drive)
  Yes, I _____ .
6 _____ Medicine? (your sister, study)
  Yes, she _____ .

will vs. be going to

3 Decide if each sentence is a plan or a prediction. Circle the correct words.
1 It's raining. You **will** / **are going to** need an umbrella.
2 I think it **will** / **is going to** be difficult to find a job.
3 The concert is sold out. You **won't** / **aren't going to** get tickets.
4 We **will** / **are going to** study Japanese next year.
5 Suzanne **will** / **is going to** work as a scientist.
6 You're an excellent student. I'm sure you **will** / **are going to** pass the test.

4 Complete the sentences with the correct form of *will* or *be going to*.
1 My cousin _is going to get_ (get) married next year.
2 Our teacher _____ (come) to class today. She's busy.
3 I _____ (study) Maths at university. I love numbers.
4 _____ (you/watch) the film tonight?
5 We _____ (play) football later. We've got a lot of homework.
6 What _____ your friends _____ (do) when they leave school?

Present continuous for future

5 Write sentences with the words. Use the present continuous.
1 I / cook dinner tonight
  I'm cooking dinner tonight.
2 Hillary / look after / her sister tomorrow
  _____
3 My dad / make / a cake for my birthday
  _____
4 He / sell / his car next week
  _____
5 We / play / basketball on Friday
  _____
6 They / do / the shopping this afternoon
  _____

6 Read Leila, Danny and Suzanne's plans and complete the table with answers about you. Then use the information to write questions and answers with the present continuous.

	Leila	Danny and Suzanne	You
Tonight	study for a test	eat pizza with their friends	_____
This weekend	visit her grandma	watch a football match	_____

1 What / Leila / do / tonight ?
  What is Leila doing tonight ?
  She's _studying for a test_ .
2 What / Danny and Suzanne / this weekend ?
  _____ ? They _____ .
3 Leila / visit / her auntie / this weekend
  _____ ? _____ .
4 Danny and Suzanne / watch a football match / this weekend ?
  _____ ? _____ .
5 you / study for a test / tonight ?
  _____ ? _____ .
6 you / watch a football match / this weekend ?
  _____ ? _____ .

Language focus extra

Present perfect: affirmative and negative

1 **Complete the sentences with the present perfect form of the verbs in brackets.**

1 Gemma _has broken_ her ankle. (break)
2 Kate _____ Colombia. (visit)
3 I _____ octopus. (not eat)
4 My brother _____ a new computer game. (invent)
5 We _____ the latest *Hobbit* film. (not see)
6 My parents _____ me a new bicycle. (buy)
7 They _____ to London twice. (go)
8 Some of my classmates _____ this book. (read)

Spelling: past participles

2 **Complete the table with the past participle of each verb.**

~~jump~~ slip trip stop study like try

Add -d or -ed	Remove the last letter and add -ied	Double consonant and add -ed
1 _jumped_	3 _____	5 _____
2 _____	4 _____	6 _____
		7 _____

Present perfect: irregular verbs

3 **Write the past participle of each verb.**

1 have _____ *had* _____
2 fall _____
3 feel _____
4 write _____
5 eat _____
6 see _____
7 begin _____
8 break _____

Present perfect: questions

4 **Write questions and short answers with the present perfect.**

1 have an accident / you
Have you had an accident _____ ?
No, I ___ *haven't* ___ .
2 Annie / ever / fall off her bike
_____ ?
Yes, she _____ .
3 Tony / break his leg
_____ ?
No, he _____ .
4 ever / they / win the lottery
_____ ?
No, they _____ .
5 she / burn / her finger
_____ ?
Yes, _____ .
6 ever / the dog / bite / you
_____ ?
No, it _____ .

Past simple vs. present perfect

5 **Circle the correct words.**

1 I visited / have visited a lot of countries in my life.
2 Sam **broke** / **has broken** his wrist two years ago.
3 Ruth **crashed** / **has crashed** her bike yesterday.
4 I **didn't eat** / **haven't eaten** snails but I want to try them one day.
5 We **didn't ride** / **haven't ridden** a camel when we were in Egypt.
6 **A:** Do you like skiing?
   B: I don't know. I **didn't do** / **haven't done** it before.

6 **Complete the story with the correct form of the verbs in brackets.**

I ¹___ *went* ___ (go) ice skating yesterday. I ²_____ (put on) big socks and the skates and ³_____ (walk) on to the ice, but of course I ⁴_____ (slip). I ⁵_____ never _____ (break) my leg but I ⁶_____ (think) I had when I ⁷_____ (fall)! Ow! I ⁸_____ (stand up) and I ⁹_____ (fall) again. This time I ¹⁰_____ (cut) my finger with the skate. I think football is much safer!

Language focus extra

one/ones

1 Circle the correct words.

1 **A:** Which T-shirt would you like, pink or blue?
   B: I'd like the blue **one** / ones, please.
2 **A:** Which biscuits would you like, chocolate or lemon?
   B: I'd like the chocolate **one** / **ones**, please.
3 **A:** What kind of ticket do you want?
   B: Which **one** / **ones** is the cheapest?
4 **A:** I really like those kinds of films.
   B: Which **one** / **ones**?
   A: Action films.
5 **A:** Which restaurant do you like best?
   B: The **one** / **ones** on the corner near the park.
6 **A:** Do you want the same flowers as last time?
   B: No, I'd like different **one** / **ones**, please.

Indefinite pronouns

2 Choose the correct words.

Edinburgh is an amazing city. [1]**Someone** / **Something** once said that it's the world capital of festivals. There's always [2]**something** / **somewhere** to do there. In the summer it has the biggest arts festival in the world. There are thousands of events [3]**everything** / **everywhere** in the city. The shows in the theatres can be expensive but many of the open-air [4]**one** / **ones** are free. In winter, the Scottish New Year party is a three-day festival, another [5]**one** / **ones** that [6]**nowhere** / **no one** wants to miss.

3 Complete the sentences with the words in the box.

nothing (x2)   something   nobody   anything
somewhere   anyone

1 Is there __anything__ in this plastic bag?
2 I'd like to go _____ very warm for my holidays!
3 I'm sorry, but there's _____ we can do to help you.
4 I don't know _____ who has a fishing boat.
5 We looked for our friends in the kitchen but there was _____ there.
6 Put all your work on this memory stick. It's OK, there's _____ on it.
7 Can I have _____ to drink please?

too + adjective

4 Complete the sentences with *too* and the words in the box.

tired   big   old   late   small   cold   excited

1 Your computer's __too old__ to have apps.
2 My desk is _____ to put all these books on.
3 I'm _____ to go out. I want to sleep!
4 That's the best news ever! I'm _____ to speak!
5 It's _____ to have a shower. It's after midnight.
6 It's _____ to go to the beach. Let's go shopping instead.
7 This laptop is _____ to take to school. I need a smaller one.

(not) adjective + enough

5 Match the sentence halves.

1 The wardrobe wasn't big enough **f**
2 My dad says I'm not old enough
3 He's good enough at football
4 The paper bag wasn't strong enough
5 The snow isn't thick enough
6 He's intelligent enough

a to play for Chelsea.
b to hold all the shopping.
c to go camping alone.
d to become an astronaut.
e to go skiing.
f to put all her clothes in.

too or enough?

6 Choose the correct option.

1 The shelf wasn't **too strong** / strong enough to hold all my books.
2 The memory stick was **too small** / **small enough** to save all the photos.
3 The dog was **too fast** / **fast enough** to catch and he ran away.
4 The ball was **too heavy** / **heavy enough** to throw. I couldn't pick it up.
5 He says he's **too good** / **not good enough** to play the piano in the concert.
6 I was **too tired** / **tired enough** to get up so I stayed in bed.
7 I'm **too old** / **not old enough** to drive.

Thanks and acknowledgments

The authors and publishers would like to thank a number of people whose support has proved invaluable during the planning, writing and production process of this course.

We would like to thank Diane Nicholls for researching and writing the Get it Right pages.

We would like to thank the following for their contributions: Emma Heyderman for writing the Language focus extra starter page and Andrew Juraschek and Ruth Cox for editorial work.

We would also like to thank the teams of educational consultants, representatives and managers working for Cambridge University Press in various countries around the world.

The authors and publishers are grateful to the following contributors:

Blooberry: concept design
emc design limited: text design and layouts
QBS Learning: photo selection
emc design limited: cover design
David Morritt and Ian Harker - DSound: audio recordings

Development of this publication has made use of the Cambridge English Corpus (CEC). The CEC is a computer database of contemporary spoken and written English, which currently stands at over one billion words. It includes British English, American English and other varieties of English. It also includes the Cambridge Learner Corpus, developed in collaboration with the University of Cambridge ESOL Examinations. Cambridge University Press has built up the CEC to provide evidence about language use that helps to produce better language teaching materials.

The publishers are grateful to the following for permission to reproduce copyright photographs and material:

p. 3 (BR): Alamy/©Stockbroker/MBI; p. 6 (BL): Shutterstock Images/Jacek Chabraszewski; p. 7 (CR): Alamy/©Ian Pilbeam; p. 8 (TR): Alamy/©Tetra Images; p. 9 (TR): Corbis/Image Source; p. 10 (B): Alamy/©Jose Luis Pelaez Inc/Blend Images; p. 11 (T): AP Images/Paul Brown/Rex Features; p. 12 (L): Shutterstock Images/discpicture; p. 12 (TR): ©David L. Moore – Lifestyle; p. 19 (BR): Shutterstock Images/Bryan Busovicki; p. 21 (TC): REX/Ken McKay; p. 21 (1): REX/Steve Meddle; p. 21 (2): REX/Ken McKay/Thames; p. 21 (3): Alamy/©Mar Photographics; p. 22 (TL): Alamy/©Ian Shaw; p. 29 (BR): Alamy/©Catchlight Visual Services; p. 31 (T): Newscom/Quique Curbelow/Epa; p. 32 (T): AP Images/Steven Senne; p. 37 (1): Shutterstock Images/Winston Link; p. 37 (2): Shutterstock Images/fokusgood; p. 37 (3): Alamy/©Martin Wierink; p. 37(4): Margo Harrison/Shutterstock; p. 37 (5): Alamy/©DJC; p. 37 (6): Shutterstock Images/Baloncici; p. 37 (7): Shutterstock Images/Elena Elisseeva; p. 37 (8): Shutterstock Images/Venus Angel; p. 37 (9): Shutterstock Images/Sergey Karpov; p. 37 (10): Alamy/©Tyson Ellis/Built Images; p. 37 (11): Shutterstock Images/Simon Bratt; p. 38 (TR): Getty/Bloomberg; p. 39 (2): Shutterstock Images/Africa Studio; p. 39 (3): Shutterstock Images/Photoseeker; p. 39 (7): Shutterstock Images/Maxal Tamor; p. 39 (8): Shutterstock Images/Mats; p. 41 (TL): Shutterstock Images/Lilly Trott; p. 41 (CL): Alamy/©Tim Gaíney; p. 41 (BL): Alamy/©Adams Picture Library t/a apl; p. 42 (L): Getty/Anthony Collins; p. 43 (TR): Alamy/©Image Source; p. 43 (CR): Alamy/©Ian Dagnall; p. 43 (CL): Alamy/©Imagestate Media Partners Limited - Impact Photos; p. 43 (BL): Shutterstock Images/Kwiatek7;vp. 47 (7): Alamy/©Henry George Beeker; p. 47 (8): Shutterstock Images/windu; p. 47 (9): Alamy/©acek Lasa;vp. 49 (CR): Alamy/©Dream Pictures/Blend Images; p. 51 (CL): Alamy/©Jim West; p. 51 (BL): Alamy/©Caryn Becker; p. 55 (TL): Corbis/Marc Romanelli/Blend Images; p. 57 (1): Rex features/Theo Kingma; p. 57 (2): Rex features/Theo Kingma; p. 57 (3): Rex features/Everett Collection; p. 57 (4): Rex features/Masatoshi Okauchi; p. 59 (TR): Superstock/ Minden Pictures; p. 59 (CR): Alamy/©dpa picture alliance archive; p. 60 (T): Alamy/©Mark Thomas; p. 61 (TR): Alamy/©Beyond Fotomedia GmbH; p. 61 (CL): Shutterstock Images/Irina Schmidt; p. 62 (T): Corbis/Nancy Ney; p. 68 (TL): Superstock/ChameleonsEye; p. 68 (TR): Corbis/Superstock; p. 68 (BL): Alamy/©Paul Carstairs; p. 68 (BR): Alamy/©Colin Hawkins/Cultura Creative; p. 69 (1): Alamy/©ROYER Philippe/SAGAPHOTO.COM; p. 69 (2): Getty/Mike Harrington; p. 69 (3): Shutterstock Images/Vitalii Nesterchuk; p. 69 (4): Shutterstock Images/abaghda; p. 71 (C): Superstock/Minden Pictures;

p. 71 (BL): Superstock/Minden Pictures; p. 71 (BC): Alamy/©John Warburton-Lee Photography; p. 72 (TL): Alamy/©PHOVOIR; p. 73 (TL): Shutterstock Images/kearia; p. 73 (BC): Shutterstock Images/TanjaJovicic; p. 73 (TR): Shutterstock Images/newcorner; p. 77 (TL): Alamy/©Dmitriy Shironosov; p. 77 (TC): Alamy/©Chris Ryan/OJO Images Ltd; p. 77 (TL): Alamy/©Bubbles Photolibrary; p. 77 (CL): Alamy/©Greg Balfour Evans; p. 77 (C): Alamy/©DreamPictures/Blend Images; p. 77 (CR): Superstock; p. 77 (BR): Alamy/©Myrleen Pearson; p. 77 (BCR): Alamy/©Frederic Cirou/PhotoAlto; p. 77 (BCL): Alamy/©Pablo Paul; p. 77 (BL): Alamy/©Tetra Images; p. 81 (TL): Alamy/©Philimages; p. 81 (C): Alamy/©Imran Ahmed; p. 81 (CL): Alamy/©fenghuai dong; p. 81 (B): Alamy/©John Crowe; p.82 (T): Shutterstock Images/magicinfoto; p.85 (TL): Shutterstock Images/lornet; p.87 (CL): Alamy/©Helene Rogers/Art Directors & TRIP; p.88 (TL): Alamy/©Patricia Phillips; p. 88 (TR): Shutterstock Images/Africa Studio; p.88 (BR): Shutterstock Images/soloir; p.88 (BL): Shutterstock Images/A and N photography; p.89 (CR): Shutterstock Images/prudkov.

The publishers are grateful to the following illustrators:

David Belmonte (Beehive Illustration) p. 28, 30; Alberto de Hoyos: p. 17, 24, 34, 67, 75, 79; Nigel Dobbyn p. 19; Mark Draisey p. 25; Mark Duffin p. 4, 47, 49, 64; emc p. 14; Jose Rubio p. 5; David Shephard: p. 4, 27, 74; Norbert Sipos (Beehive Illustration) p. 17, 39, 48, 59, 64, 69, 70; Sean Tiffany p. 24, 50, 80.